PRAISE FOR
Small Business, Big Success

"I have read hundreds of books in the entrepreneurial ecosystem designed to help entrepreneurs build and scale businesses. This book should be at the top of the list for any entrepreneur looking to learn from the experiences of others to fully understand the exhilarating journey from startup to successful exit. This book contains wisdom from people who have been there, done that. This book is a true treasure for the entrepreneurial community. This book, quite simply, rocks!"

—**DAVID GALBENSKI**, serial entrepreneur, past global chair of the Entrepreneurs' Organization, and cofounder and chair of the Global School of Entrepreneurship

"From our experience at the Edward Lowe Foundation, Cynthia Kay is one of the best and brightest entrepreneurs in Michigan. This book shares her success story and is chockful of leadership lessons that address a broad spectrum of small-business challenges, from startup to succession planning. What also makes this book a great read is its relevancy: Kay looks at how the small-business landscape has significantly changed in recent years, from aftershocks of the pandemic to shifts in the economy."

—**DAN WYANT**, chairman and president of the Edward Lowe Foundation

"Whether you've got an idea ready to grow or are looking for inspiration to take a new step in your business, this book will ignite your entrepreneurial spirit. Cynthia Kay shares her own wisdom, and that of fellow entrepreneurs, through candid anecdotes, practical advice, and thought-provoking reflections. What a fantastic resource for businesses of all stages."

—**BRIAN CALLEY**, president and CEO, Small Business Association of Michigan

"Entrepreneurship is in Cynthia Kay's DNA! In *Small Business, Big Success*, Cynthia provides a roadmap for anyone who wants to start (or grow) their own business. The lessons on these pages are filled with essential strategies and tactics that are born through the experience and wisdom of a seasoned professional. *Small Business, Big Success* should be required reading for all MBA students; and is a complete gift for business owners of all sizes."

—**TERRI DEBOER**, meteorologist and
lifestyle-show host; author of *Encore Season,
Grieving Well,* and *Brighter Skies Ahead*

"Cynthia's new book arrives at the perfect time. Small business is tough. It's not for the faint of heart. The past few years have clearly shown it. Take the wisdom, lessons, and tips in the book and apply them to your own business. Having been self-employed for nearly twenty years, I picked up several tips and ways to improve my own business. Use Cynthia's thirty-five-plus-year track record of success in this excellent book to guide and mentor you along the small business journey. Bravo, Cynthia!"

—**TONY RUBLESKI**, bestselling author and
entrepreneur, *MindCaptureGroup.com*

"Cynthia's conversational style makes this book easy to read and understand while still providing real-life anecdotes that are as intriguing as they are illustrative. Her own successful move from broadcasting to small business entrepreneur gives her the unique ability to effectively communicate how her valuable strategies can help any small business owner beat the odds and grow their company. This book tackles everything a small business owner needs to know, from start-up to stimulus to stepping down."

—**HEATHER RIPLEY**, CEO RipleyPR, author
of *Next Level Now: PR Secrets to Drive Explo-
sive Growth for Your Home Service Business*

SMALL BUSINESS,

BIG

SUCCESS

PROVEN STRATEGIES TO BEAT THE ODDS AND
GROW A GREAT BUSINESS

Cynthia Kay

Foreword by Todd McCracken

 CAREER PRESS

This edition first published in 2024 by Career Press, an imprint of
Red Wheel/Weiser, LLC

With offices at:
65 Parker Street, Suite 7
Newburyport, MA 01950
www.careerpress.com
www.redwheelweiser.com

ISBN: 978-1-63265-213-3

Library of Congress Cataloging-in-Publication Data

Names: Kay, Cynthia, 1953- author. | McCracken, Todd, writer of foreword.
Title: Small business, big success : proven strategies to beat the odds and
    grow a great business / Cynthia Kay ; foreword by Todd McCracken.
Description: Newburyport, MA : Career Press, 2024. | Includes index. |
    Summary: "An invaluable resource for those starting a new business or
    veterans looking for a better way, this book offers unconventional but
    proven strategies to run a better small business. It also provides a
    roadmap for owners looking to expand their small business by doing more
    business with Big Business."-- Provided by publisher.
Identifiers: LCCN 2023049451 | ISBN 9781632652133 (trade paperback) | ISBN
    9781632652140 (ebook)
Subjects: LCSH: Small business--Management. | Big business. | BISAC:
    BUSINESS & ECONOMICS / Small Business | BUSINESS & ECONOMICS /
    Entrepreneurship
Classification: LCC HD62.7 .K387 2024 | DDC 658.4/012--dc23/eng/20231102

LC record available at https://lccn.loc.gov/2023049451

Cover design by Brittany Craig
Interior by Happenstance Type-O-Rama
Typeset in Forma DJR Display, RBNo2.1a, Soleil, and Warnock Pro

Printed in the United States of America
IBI

10 9 8 7 6 5 4 3 2 1

This book is dedicated to entrepreneurs of all ages who take on the challenge of business ownership. I am inspired by you and hope this book will help move you even further along your journey.

CONTENTS

SECTION 3: SUCCEED AT GROWTH

SECTION 4: SUCCEED AT STEPPING OUT

FOREWORD

Over the past thirty-five years working with and for small-business owners, I can attest to the very strong drive innate in all of them, but few have the kind of strategic vision of Cynthia Kay. Cynthia has been active on NSBA's board and various committees for nearly twenty years, and she has made an indelible mark on the organization.

As the nation's longest running small-business advocacy organization, NSBA (National Small Business Association) serves as an external government affairs shop for the millions of small businesses who can't afford their own. We have 65,000 members in every state and every industry across the nation, and we are proud to have been representing America's small businesses on Capitol Hill since 1937.

One thing that makes NSBA so unique is that we are staunchly nonpartisan, beholden to nobody but our small-business members. As politics have become more contentious, our leadership has been able to bring together small-business leaders of all political stripes for the common good.

Serving as our board chair in 2018, Cynthia played a critical role in our five-year strategic planning process and was a champion for NSBA creating a new group for emerging small-business leaders called the NSBA Leadership Council. Five years later, that council has nearly one thousand members and is extremely engaged and active. Cynthia embodies the spirit of who we are: a solution-oriented organization focused on small business and dedicated to consensus building.

Not only was Cynthia a pragmatic leader while in numerous leadership roles here at NSBA, she and her team developed a series of marketing videos that are still relevant and highly utilized.

Small-business advocacy can be a curious thing. On the one hand, every politician espouses their strong support for small business; the reality of that, however, is that when push comes to shove in Congress, small business is often an afterthought.

As you will read—small business is big business. There are seventy million people in the US who work for or run a small business—that's one out of every four people. Nearly half of all private sector employees are in small business, and 99 percent of all US firms are small businesses. We—you—matter, and it's through organizations like NSBA and advocates like Cynthia Kay that your voice can be heard.

It hasn't always been comfortable being a long-time staffer with Cynthia in leadership. But that's what makes her so important. She has forced NSBA, and me personally, to look at things differently, to examine our mission, how we attain that mission, and how we can do better.

To have a force like Cynthia on your side—even when it may push you beyond your comfort zone—is akin to harnessing the wind. As a beloved author once said, "Oh the places you'll go . . ."

> *Todd McCracken is president and CEO of the National Small Business Association, the nation's first small-business advocacy organization, operating on a staunchly nonpartisan basis with more than 65,000 members in every state and every nation in the country.*

ACKNOWLEDGMENTS

It is a simple truth. No one gets anywhere in business or life without the help and support of others. I am blessed to have so many in my personal and professional life who have been my guides, my mentors, my heroes. My sister, Vicki, and her husband, Charles, have played all three of these roles. They cared for our parents day to day until they both passed away. During much of the time, they were also running an impressive small business. They have been an inspiration with how they managed their business and their exit. My thanks go out to the staff at Cynthia Kay and Company. These are individuals who share my love of small business, and they prove it every day. Special thanks to Todd McCracken and all of the staff at the National Small Business Association, and Colleen Killen-Roberts at the Edward Lowe Foundation. Their assistance goes far beyond their contribution to this book.

My writing journey has had starts and stops as I navigated trying to assist with ailing parents, grow a business, and serve on boards of organizations that advocate for small business. Let's face it, there is only so much time. I am fortunate that my amazing agent, John Willig, stuck with me. He helped find a place for my first book, *Small Business for Big Thinkers,* with Career Press. He also saw the vision for this book and once again worked with Michael Pye at Career Press on this project. I am truly grateful to both John and Michael because I know how much competition there is in the publishing world.

There are others I want to acknowledge. Without my customers and fellow small-business owners, there would be no book. Every person I contacted to provide content said yes and was generous with their time. Thanks to Bonnie Alfonso, Jack Buchanan, Bob Fish, John Kowalski, Marilyn Landis, Christopher Locke, Yan Ness, Chad Paalman, Mark Peters, Tom Price, and

Linda Schlesinger-Wagner for all their stories. I did not even know Kenneth Marks, but he responded to an email for help and was a great resource. Sandra Jelinski of Lake Michigan Credit Union also responded, and her contribution is much appreciated. Other advisors have been Tess Woods and Alicia Simons. Both of them have helped me craft my plan for this book and so much more.

My thanks to all, you know how much you mean to me. Stay tuned because I have already started authoring the next book. I think you will love it.

INTRODUCTION

BROADCASTER TO BUSINESS OWNER

This book is based upon my experience as the owner of a small business that has attracted some well-known and respected large customers. It's an award-winning media production and communication company. But my experience in business began long before I started the company; it began in the backroom of a dry-cleaning establishment. It was a family-owned business operated by three brothers, the descendants of Greek immigrants. The brothers also owned a small burger joint right next door where the specialty was—what else?—Greek chili dogs.

I can remember working at the cleaners from the time I was old enough to follow directions. Every Saturday, Dad would take my sister, younger brother, and me to the store. While he did paperwork or caught up on loads of clothing in need of attention, we would check in the dirty clothes, put paper inserts on hangers, and clean the store. That was my first foray into business, and, believe me, there was no better feeling than having the run of the store. As I got older, I worked my way up to being a counter girl, my first sales experience. Then I was able to open and close the place, my first management experience.

My parents were definitely ahead of their time. In an era when most Greek parents wanted their daughters to "get married and have babies" (yes, that famous line from *My Big Fat Greek Wedding* is very accurate), my parents wanted us to go to school, get educated, and have careers. But to be clear, my dad did not want us to go into the family business; he wanted us to achieve more. So, we did.

My sister, Vicki, along with her husband, Charles, owned a boutique rental company in Raleigh, North Carolina. You'll hear more about them in this book. My brother, Steve, is a successful lawyer. As for me, I went to Michigan State University, became a broadcaster, and then got my master's degree. No overachievers in this family.

For more than ten years, I had a successful, award-winning career in broadcast journalism. I did it all; from anchoring, producing, directing, and hosting specialty programming to investigative reporting, documentaries, and features. In the process, I was honored with more than thirty awards from United Press International and the Associated Press, plus numerous regional and local broadcast awards. Pardon the bragging, but you'll see how working in broadcasting helped me when you read chapter 9. I got tired of working for a TV station where the owners changed every year or so—and so did the priorities! Every new owner seemed more focused on cost cutting and less concerned about the quality of the product and the needs of the local community. By the way, I got fired, but that is a topic for a whole other book.

It was time to make a change. Like countless others, I dreamed about having more control over my life and career. I wanted to own my own business, run it, and grow it. That's why I founded Cynthia Kay and Company, and for over thirty-five years the business has thrived.

Today, CK and CO serves corporations from the Global Fortune 100, as well as small businesses and nonprofit organizations. Our clients are pretty impressive, including Siemens Industry, Dematic, Wiley Publishing, Nestlé, Cisco Technologies, Bradford White, the International Society of Primerus Law Firms, and countless others.

The strategies I am about to share are a major reason for our success. It's a simple but often misunderstood fact. A small business is not just a scaled-down version of a big business. Some of the strategies that work well for larger companies may actually be counterproductive for smaller firms.

Small Business, Big Success provides proven strategies to achieve success from starting up to stepping out. They are logical, clear, understandable, and easy to act upon. The early chapters help lay the foundation for what it takes to build and grow a small business that is healthy, efficient, and a great place to work. If you don't get this right, you will become a statistic—one of the many businesses that does not make it past the five-year mark.

Strategies like "Get Smart about Partnering" (chapter 4) or "You Are the Boss. Now What?" (chapter 7) get you off to a great start. In the later chapters, the book provides a roadmap for small companies looking to expand their businesses by doing business with big business. Trust me; it isn't as easy as it sounds. "The Big Business Buyer's Perspective" (chapter 14), "Create Brand Fanatics and Nurture Them" (chapter 16), along with "Give Something Away, Get More Business" (chapter 19), show you how to connect and deepen the relationship with customers and also give back to the community. Because I believe in seeing the whole picture, there are chapters to help you begin to think about "success at stepping out." Each chapter ends with Tips to Succeed.

By sharing my own experiences, from growing up in a family business to running my own media production company, along with the experiences of others, I aim to provide the kind of information and inspiration that will help small-business owners. A fellow business owner told me that her favorite saying is, "Small businesses are not small because we are too stupid to be big." I agree and would add that you don't need to have lots of employees and mega-facilities to have a big impact. Read on.

SUCCEED AT STARTING UP

1
SMALL BUSINESS, BIG SUCCESS

For some, it is a lifelong dream. Starting a business, taking over a family business, or buying an already established one. For others, stepping into the role of business owner is a necessity due to an extended layoff or complete job loss. Whatever the reason, here are some facts.

According to the Small Business Administration (SBA), there are 32.5 million small businesses in the United States, and they employ 46.8 percent of the country's private sector workforce. Even more amazing, today the majority of Americans want to work for themselves. In 2022 in the United States, over five million new businesses started. This is a record number of new small businesses. Those who start businesses are, not surprisingly, millennials and Gen Zers, who make up the greatest percentage, followed closely by Gen Xers. Bottom line—after years of negative small business growth, the tide is changing.

In many ways, it is easier than ever to start a business. Technology has advanced. The internet has made it simpler to market, sell, and distribute products and services. Individuals with great ideas can crack niche markets or overtake giant brands.

Entrepreneurs of All Ages

Entrepreneurs are individuals with great ideas. Those ideas come to them at all ages. Communities across the country have award programs for "30 under 30" or "40 under 40." These award winners include young business owners. But much younger people are also starting businesses. You sometimes see them accompanied by a parent on *Shark Tank*. In fact, in Season 5, the show had a "Young Entrepreneurs" special.

Young people may not even know they are starting a business. According to *Business News Daily*,[1] Alina Morse, founder of Zolli Candy, got the idea for her business at the age of seven when offered a lollipop at the local bank. She knew that sugar was not good for you and started working on a treat that would be good for her teeth. Hannah Grace started BeYOUtiful (not to be confused with BeYOUtiful Foundation) when her father challenged her to make her own bath bombs. EvanTubeHD, aka Evan Moana, appeared on his father's YouTube channel and then started his own. It has over seven million subscribers. While all of these young people are impressive, you might even say fearless, what is perhaps even more impressive is starting a business toward the "end of your runway in life."

Linda Schlesinger-Wagner is also fearless. She started her business, skinnytees, at the age of sixty-one, a time when many think of retiring. During a difficult transition from a divorce, the business became a reality. Schlesinger-Wagner had worked in the fashion industry and designed women's clothing. But this was different. This was her own enterprise and her simple idea to create a line of products for women of all sizes, all different ages and shapes, has garnered her national attention on QVC, *Good Morning America*, and at retailers and online. Schlesinger-Wagner says:

> I thought of skinnytees in the middle of the night. I had no money. I had a little tiny house. I had a mortgage to pay. I was working four or five part-time jobs, very part time. I lay in bed and cried many nights, but I had to support myself. Retiring? That never crossed my mind. I'm fortunate because I made it work. Failure wasn't an option. I didn't need a lot. The truth is you don't need a lot. We all have a lot. It's just stuff. So, I wanted to bring something to women to make them feel good. And the truth is, while I was making them feel good, I felt good.[2]

There is no doubt that entrepreneurs have passion and drive. Otherwise, why would they risk starting a business when the odds of succeeding are admittedly terrible. I believe that entrepreneurs of all ages have much to offer. Young entrepreneurs can bring a fresh perspective to business. They are not hampered or weighed down by history. Instead, they are curious and imaginative. They can deliver a little twist or a true innovation to a traditional industry. Or invent a whole new one. If young entrepreneurs fail, as many do, the reality is they have lots of time to start over. On the other hand, older entrepreneurs have less time to recover from setbacks, but those who have been in the working world for some time bring a depth of experience that is priceless.

For Linda Schlesinger-Wagner, that experience has provided insight into an extremely competitive business and the ability to help guide others. She says, "What I have on my side is a lot of years in business, making money, losing money. I've done it all. You learn from every mistake and bad judgment call. I'm seventy-five and I'm still learning. But I just do it. I think we should all help each other. Someone calls me and they're starting a business, I'll help in any way I can."[3]

Something else that entrepreneurs have in common is the drive to constantly develop new products and do business with big well-known businesses and media outlets. They also have a commitment and desire to give back. You will hear more about that in chapter 19.

A Love/Hate Relationship

I believe there has always been a love/hate relationship between small business and big business. Big businesses get tired of being called slow and inefficient. They hate it when small business is called the backbone of the American economy. Small-business owners will tell you that big business gets all the breaks, special treatment, and legislation to help them compete. They say everyone only *talks* about being a friend to small business. Year after year, politicians give speeches about the importance of small business to job creation and innovation, but many do nothing to help reduce the tax burdens and regulations. The truth is, small business always has been and is the "darling" of the business world, the little engine that could.

When most of us think about a small business, we think about a local retailer, a restaurant owner, a service provider, or a small manufacturing company. But the true definition of a small business, according to the SBA, is "one with either fewer than five hundred employees or net assets under a specific dollar amount of after-tax net income for the previous two years." There is also a classification called the "micro business." That is a company that has nine or fewer employees.

No matter what the size of the small business, I have found them to be fiercely proud that they are small. But here is something else I have observed. Small businesses can do big business if they take the time to study their target market and do it right from the ground up.

Why Big Businesses Like Small Businesses

Big businesses were my very first customers. It was in working with them that I realized why they, and customers of all sizes, love small business.

- **We are easy to do business with.** We are not likely to have a whole legal staff that wants to negotiate every single point of a contract. We don't have complicated processes and procedures that have to be researched and adhered to.

- **We respond quickly.** Our organizations are flexible. We can move schedules around, assign people to step in when needed, and we don't have an 8 a.m. to 5 p.m. mentality. If you need us, we are there, sometimes 24/7.

- **We can change course when needed without having to consult endless gatekeepers.** If the scope of a project changes, we adapt. If we need to buy equipment or inventory to accommodate a change, we don't have to wait to get approvals that might stall the work.

- **We bring them great new ideas.** We love to create new things instead of doing things the way they have always been done. We get excited by new challenges.

- **We believe that we can make things happen, so we do.** My favorite phrase is "it is doable." We find ways to pull off even the most difficult projects.

▸ **Finally, because we are "lean," we provide great value and don't waste their time or money.** Small-business owners spend their client's money as if it were their own. I routinely advise my big clients that they are asking me to do something that will cost them money unnecessarily. They appreciate that.

For these reasons, and many more, businesses of all sizes like to work with small businesses. At least, that's what I think. But I decided to test my theory on a few of my big customers, fellow small-business owners, and others. Many of those I reached out to have worked for both large and small businesses.

Bigger Is Not Necessarily Better

Marilyn Landis is one small-business owner who understands both sides of the small business/big business landscape. She worked for three of the largest Small Business Association lenders in the country. She currently runs her own small business, Basic Business Concepts, Inc.

> Some businesses function best as small businesses, but that does not mean we are not very sophisticated or that we don't have very complex systems. We are sophisticated, and we do have systems in place to help us deliver flawlessly. There is a saying that I love: "those who think bigger is better and older is smarter, forget the dinosaur that got bigger, not better, and older, not smarter."[4]

Attention and Flexibility Get You Noticed

John Kowalski, director of strategic marketing for a global manufacturing company, has been my client for many years, both with his current company, and at a previous one as well. John has a unique perspective because he is also the owner of a small consulting company. As a result, he too sees both sides of the story. In his role with a large manufacturing company, he has a number of small businesses as service suppliers. When asked why he prefers them to some of the big guys, Kowalski said:

> Smaller suppliers are more attentive, more flexible, and, most importantly, they listen. They provide a noncorporate-America perspective of things. When you are on the inside of a big corporation, it is

easy to get tainted, to get sucked into that corporate mind-set. I want something to make my project better. As a result, I want a different perspective, and a smaller company can often provide that.[5]

Of course, this is not true of all small businesses. But it is true of those that are well run and forward thinking. Another reason big companies like small companies is the expertise and availability of the owner. Kowalski says:

With a big company, you get the salesperson or the account executive in to make the sale, then you never see them again. It's, "Here, I'll take that signed contract, and Bob over there will take care of you." And Bob is generally someone with a lot less experience than the person that sold me the job. I don't want to train someone. I want an expert. When I work with a small company, I get the owner and their support staff. I am getting *the* experts in that firm. The owner or managing partner has their hand in every aspect of that company. They are going to direct the work and make sure it is right. After all, their name is on the door.[6]

In my first interview for a contract with a large manufacturing company, I was a little put off by the questions. The interviewer kept asking, "And who will do the interviewing, and who will be on site, and who will I communicate with?" To every question I answered, "That would be me!" I found out later that this individual had been burned. The previous supplier had done exactly what John Kowalski described above. They got the contract and then sent in junior-level employees to do the work and, I might add, not very successfully.

The idea of expertise is especially critical in professional services. Jack Buchanan is the founder of the International Society of Primerus Law Firms, known simply as Primerus. Their firms are small to medium-sized boutique law firms. As they like to say, "good people, who happen to be good lawyers." One of the key reasons that individuals and companies choose these firms over the "big guys" is that they provide top quality work from partners at reasonable fees. Many of the lawyers who make up these firms began working for much larger ones. They made a choice to be a part of or manage a smaller entity. Buchanan says:

It is very simple. You are either working for someone else and doing it their way, or you are working for yourself and doing it your way.

Lawyers working for Big Law are just employees working for a big corporation. Lawyers working for very successful small boutique law firms have those extra qualities of highly specialized skills, self-confidence, and the entrepreneurial spirit of winners. That is why they are usually the best.[7]

Smaller does not mean that the Primerus firms can't do big business. As a part of the network, these smaller firms have access to global firms through their platform and can serve clients anywhere in the world. If you want to be a smaller entity, having a network is critical. Buchanan explains:

> The best want to be associated with the best, and Primerus is a society of the world's finest law firms. By joining together, they gain the advantage of global reach and the infrastructure of Big Law, without the disadvantages of working for someone else. Put simply, they have the best of both worlds. As Frank Sinatra used to sing, "I did it my way," and that is what it is all about.[8]

Small Businesses Love to Experiment

In addition to working directly with the business owner, bigger businesses like the entrepreneurial spirit of small companies. They like that we will experiment with them. Mark Peters, CEO of Butterball Farms, Inc., began his career working for a large company and now works with some of the biggest names in the food industry. His company is the largest national dairy supplier of specialty and premium butter in the US, but it is still a small business. Peters says:

> There's a lot more at stake for us as small business owners because once you get the business, you can't afford to lose it. Years ago, we were willing to do an experiment for a leading global food service retailer with restaurants in approximately 199 countries. They were concerned about running out of product. We were concerned about balancing the production level in our plant. So, we invested some time and money and became the pilot for a whole new Vendor Managed Inventory system that they ended up implementing. We were their first US supplier to do that. Everyone benefitted.[9]

Are You Ready to Do Big Business?

Chances are, because you are a small entity, your customers will be larger than your operation. In my case, that is certainly true. Our ten-person organization serves entities from nonprofits to global leaders. They are all bigger than my firm, and that has led to our success. So how do you know if doing business with big business is right for you? Here are a few things to ask yourself and your team before you start to court big business:

- **Are you ready for a new challenge?** Doing business with a large company won't be the same as working with smaller customers. Big customers have very different needs and expect a high level of performance.

- **Are you more forward thinking than your current customers?** Big businesses are always looking for those who can help them get ahead and give them a fresh, outside perspective, especially during tough economic times.

- **Can you ramp up your capacity if you get a huge contract?** Getting the contract is just the start. You have a lot of hard work ahead of you after that.

- **Do you have the machinery, space, people, etc., to deal with spikes in business?** You will need to find the money to make investments and have great cash flow to help you deal with the ups and downs, not to mention that many big businesses take a while to pay.

- **Do you have the technology you need?** You can't be behind in this area. Big business does not have the time to wait while you figure this out.

- **Do you have a product or service that you have perfected?** You have to be the best at what you do because you are unproven, and they are looking for a quality product.

- **Do you know how to build long-lasting relationships?** Big business does not want to spend time and money getting you into their system and educating you about their business for a one-time job. Many have been trying to reduce their supplier base and consolidate suppliers.

▸ **Are you willing to do what it takes?** The truth is big business is demanding. So be really clear on this one.

This is just the start of it. Doing business with big business is not for everyone. I know small-business owners who have actually lost money on jobs. One owner told me that a huge contract caused them to staff up only to have to lay people off when the contract was not renewed. Another said they had to grow so fast that the quality of their work suffered. You have to be ready for these contingencies.

So, what do I mean when I say that small businesses can do big business? It's no surprise that big businesses have had a rough go of it. They have downsized, and now many find themselves with staff that is overburdened. They may not have invested a lot in their operations or their people due to economic conditions, so they must play catch-up. Or, on a more positive note, they may be working to launch new products or services and are seeking out the best suppliers to help them.

In short, this is a time of opportunity, but only if you get operationally efficient, creative, and pay attention. The journey to connecting with and winning big business starts before you even open the doors and continues by running the best possible small-business operation.

TIPS TO SUCCEED

▸ There are many things that big businesses like about small businesses, including responsiveness, flexibility, and creativity.

▸ Use the checklist in this chapter to see if you are ready to do business with big business.

▸ Big business is reaching out. Look for opportunities.

2

HAVE AN EXIT STRATEGY BEFORE YOU OPEN THE DOORS

There is no doubt about it; new small businesses are springing up every day. More people than ever are motivated to pursue the American Dream of opening a small business and being the boss. What's the attraction?

Countless individuals have been downsized out of large companies. Others have simply decided to leave the corporate world in what has been called "The Great Resignation" to pursue a dream and bet on themselves. But in the rush to open the doors, many miss one important step: they forget to think about an exit strategy. This is not uncommon. Most business owners love their business. Why else would they have started it or purchased it? They love the excitement of creating something, the rush when someone buys their product or when they land a big account. Exit strategy? Why would you even want to think about it? And why now?

Simple: if you know how you want to exit, it helps determine how you build, operate, and run your small business.

Questions to Get You Thinking

Here are a few questions you need to ask yourself. They may sound elementary, but getting crystal-clear answers now will help you stay on track as you grow your business.

- What are your long-term plans for the business, assuming that you make it through those first rough years?

- Do you want partners?

- Are you thinking about growing the business quickly so you can sell it?

- Do you want to work until you are well past the age when most people retire? Or do you want to retire early? (Good luck with that one.)

- Do you want to leave your business to the next generation? Is there a family member who might be a likely buyer or manager?

- Do you want to turn your business into a franchise? If you do, how will that change your role?

Knowing what you want drives the decisions you make and the timing of your exit. Believe me—exiting from a small business can be complicated. Here are a few examples from my own experience.

Exiting a Family-Owned Business

My father's business, Afendoulis Cleaners, was owned by three brothers. It started like many family businesses—no business plan, no buy-sell agreements, and no job descriptions—just a lot of hard work, some intuition, and a bit of luck. Some would say it's a wonder that the family survived the building of the business, several downturns in the economy, and the buyout of first one brother and then another, especially considering there was no exit strategy. Like many business owners, the brothers thought that one of the children would step up. That was probably the exit strategy, but there was nothing written down.

When it came time for my dad to retire, my siblings and I did not want the business. Dad wanted to sell the business and the property, and have both brothers retire. His brother wanted to keep working. It is not uncommon that people have different timetables given their age, health, and other family dynamics.

It was time to negotiate an exit and, without an agreement in place, that is not easy. Everyone thinks they are entitled to more. Everyone thinks their contribution to the enterprise was the reason for its success. The truth is probably somewhere in the middle. In this case, each brother wanted to be sure they gave the other brother his due.

I think the negotiations were difficult. But it is a testament to the character of the individuals who started the business and our families that, to this day, the relationships are intact. Often, that is not the case.

A Lesson Learned

As much as I saw the pitfalls of business partnerships (that's a whole other lesson we'll cover later), I still thought I needed someone to complement my talents when I started my business. So, I found a partner. I knew from observing our family's business that I needed a plan and the legal documents. The buy-sell was one of the first things we addressed so that we would have an exit strategy. I thought it was important that it not be a fifty-fifty deal. Someone needed to be the lead. I was taking on a greater financial risk by using the equity in my house as collateral, so it was decided I would own 51 percent of the business, and my partner would own 49 percent.

For a number of years, things went well. Then, over time, it became obvious that we were simply not on the same path. He wanted to keep the business small, really small, and exert lots of control over every aspect of it. I wanted to grow the business—not too big but big enough so that we could attract the type of big clients and projects that would keep it interesting. I also knew that I did not want to be one of those business owners who had no work/life balance. Without extra bodies, I knew that I would have to do everything. I could not focus on attracting new business *and* moving the company forward with new products and services.

To try to reconcile our differences, my partner and I went to business counseling. We worked with a consultant for a number of sessions to see if we could find the common ground that we'd had when we started the business. It worked for a while, but soon things were right back to where we started before our attempts to save the partnership.

The options were simple: I buy him out, he buys me out, or we sell the whole thing. That last option was the least desirable because it would have taken far too long to find a buyer and make the transition. When we set up the business, we put a buy-sell agreement in place. Because there was an exit strategy, it took about eighty days from start to finish.

I bought him out and decided to sit tight and run the business. In the long run, I knew I had made the right decision not to be the one taking leave. Of course, I have continued to invest in it. That investment, along with growing the client base consisting of bigger customers, has made the business more valuable. Now I'm working on a more long-term exit strategy.

Consider Your Options at the Outset

Family-owned businesses have diverse ways of passing the business down from generation to generation. But, if you don't have family to step in, is there a group of employees that might have an interest? I know of several small businesses that have set up Employee Stock Ownership Plans (ESOP), which provide employees with stock, often at no cost to them. While this might be a great option, it can also be a little pricey for a small business to set up and administer.

You can bring in a younger employee, train them, and do a buyout over time. This helps make the transition easier for customers. It may also make the deal more attractive to banks or other lenders because the individual has knowledge of the business and has already made an investment.

Is there a competitor that could benefit by acquiring your operation? Or is there a related business that could add to their product and service offering by merging their business with yours? You might choose to use a business broker. We will talk more about successfully exiting in section 4.

No Exit Strategy: Is That a Strategy?

There is one strategy that I have not explored. It's having no exit strategy. Bob Fish is the cofounder and co-CEO of Biggby Coffee, one of the top twenty food-service franchise concepts in the nation. When I interviewed him in 2013, he said he had no exit strategy:

> I don't have one because I don't intend on exiting. I'm not racing to some IPO [initial public offering] just so that I can rally up the stock price and get out. I am building a company for the long haul. We have had many offers to be bought, and we've entertained some of those, but we've never been interested in selling. This is not what I do so that I can have a hobby. I have built my life and my job to be intertwined so that I can still spend a lot of time with my family, pursuing other interests like travel and personal development. I really believe in a balanced lifestyle. Occasionally that gets tested. It has to be a little elastic. But what I'd like to do is build a company that survives me, and I only have so much time left on this earth to do that. My goal is not to figure out my exit strategy, but to figure out how to ensure that the company survives me. That's my legacy.[1]

So how does Fish feel years later? Does he still believe that he can continue to work and not retire? I asked and here was his unequivocal response.

> Yes, I still don't think I'm going to retire. I do want to go out with my boots on, although there have been times where crazy money has been suggested for the business. But even though that's happened, and after making so many millions, who cares? I think if this was a job, then I would use words like retirement. But one of the advantages of being an entrepreneur is that you get to have choices about how you participate in the business. And at BIGGBY, we practice the EOS [Entrepreneurial Operating System] model. Both Michael, our cofounder, and I are in the visionary role, which doesn't really involve that much tactical work. I'm not digging ditches, you know? We're looking out five to ten years and setting the strategy for the company and other folks managing the bits and pieces. Who couldn't do that for the rest of their life?[2]

After hearing that and seeing firsthand the passion that Fish has for his company, I think that not having an exit strategy is also a strategy. While I really like the idea of a company living on—and I want that same thing for my company—you have to put a lot of thought into how to make that happen. You will need a solid business model and trusted people at various levels of the company to "work it," because the reality is that most people just can't keep working at the same pace as they move into their later years. Of course, there is always an exception, and Bob Fish might be one. But none of us will live forever, so work with legal counsel to handle how to pass on the shares or ownership of the company, sell it, or simply liquidate the assets.

Should You Close the Doors?

Another option for exiting a business is to just close the doors. While this seems drastic, it happens repeatedly. There are a number of factors that influence this decision. I have seen businesses that could no longer afford the space they had rented due to increases in rent or lack of sales. One business closed up shop because it had invested too much in the development of a new product that never launched. Some have difficulty finding and retaining staff. I know of another small business that lost a major client, more than 60 percent of their sales, and that was enough to force them to shut down. Diversification is paramount. But many ignore this reality, lose an important client, and then must make the decision to close the doors before the expenses start to pile up.

A Few Final Thoughts

If you are a sole proprietor in a service business, you are especially vulnerable. You are the business. You have the relationships and deliver the service. If you can no longer work, there is really nothing to sell except goodwill or a list, and that just does not go very far.

If you're starting a business, be sure you think about an exit strategy and know that it might change over time. If you own a business and do not have a strategy, it's not too late—start now. If you have a strategy but it no longer makes good business sense, revisit it and develop a new one that does. We will talk about this in much more detail in the closing chapter.

TIPS TO SUCCEED

▸ When you start to plan an exit strategy, get legal assistance and don't skimp. A good lawyer saves you time and money in the long run.

▸ Create a detailed exit strategy with a number of scenarios and reevaluate them regularly.

▸ Let key customers and employees know what you are doing. Don't surprise them with big organizational changes; it makes them very nervous.

3
DO YOU HAVE PASSION AND STAYING POWER?

assion. It's the one thing that I believe every entrepreneur has regardless of their business or industry. Over the years, I have seen business owners get excited about everything from pallets (yes, really!) to new software platforms. The excitement literally oozes from every pore. They talk enthusiastically about the product or service they are developing or selling. They gush about the market potential.

Anthony Robbins put it beautifully when he said, "There is no greatness without a passion to be great, whether it's the aspiration of an athlete or an artist, a scientist, a parent, or a businessperson."

The Relationship between Passion and Success

Consider some of the words that the thesaurus equates to "passionate"— afire, heated, intense, stimulated, activated, zealous, energized, vibrant, fervent, and spirited. You get the idea? This describes an energetic, engaged, and active person. A person who makes things happen. There is a direct relationship between passion and success. The more passionate the individual, the greater the likelihood of success.

Why? It's simple—when you love what you do, you spend more time doing it. And you do it in a way that is authentic. That applies to all aspects of the business. Small-business owners wear a lot of hats. There are some things that we prefer to do, but we are willing to do whatever it takes—from sweeping the floors and working on the line to taking out second mortgages on homes to keep the business afloat.

I know that I care so much about my business that I will do anything and work ridiculous hours to be successful. It is common for business owners to miss family events, stay late or work weekends, go years without a real vacation. When a last-minute request pops up at my office, it is a challenge to see if I can fulfill it. Getting on a plane to visit a customer or taking a road trip is an adventure not a burden. It is passion that drives me to work hard every day.

Tracy Brower, the author of *The Secrets to Happiness at Work* and *Bring Work to Life by Bringing Life to Work*, believes that passion for one's work is different for every individual. Brower says:

> Ask yourself, what am I excited about? What am I interested in? Where do I want to put my energy? And it is not just pushing energy out, but what am I getting back? When you have passion, you are energized. Sociologically, engagement is fundamentally about three things. It's dedication, immersion, and vigor. And I think that has a close relationship to passion. I'm dedicated to this work. I'm committed to it. I'm putting my heart into it. I'm immersed in it. There is a feeling that I am plunging into it. The work is a big part of what I think about. I'm interested in it but not imprisoned by it.[1]

Love What You Do

We all want to love what we do. Let's face it, we spend a lot of our waking hours at work. However, there is more to consider. Tracy Brower says:

> The data is really interesting. We know that if you're happy at work, you perceive more happiness outside of work. That's well known. But the thing that's not well known is the opposite is also true. If you're happy outside of work, you perceive more happiness inside of work. So you have to understand that all of the aspects of your work and life matter to your happiness.[2]

I have a sign in my office that says, "Do more of what makes you happy." There are many things that I do that make me happy. I spend time with family and friends. I direct my church choir. I golf. It also makes me very happy to work on and in my business. That is not the case with so many people. According to 2022 US job satisfaction statistics, "the number of disengaged workers is now more than 50% of all US employees. Disengaged employees are those that sleepwalk through their day without passion or energy."[3]

Many individuals who are "unhappy" at their current job are starting or buying businesses. It may be hard to describe the passion that these business owners demonstrate, but others know it when they see it, and it offers a competitive edge. I wish I had just a dime for every time someone said to me, "You really love what you do." That passion is infectious with several audiences.

People want to work for companies and individuals that love what they do. When a business owner can eagerly articulate the mission and value of the company, it makes employees feel more secure about their future. They see how committed the owner is to the business and the success of the organization. That goes a long way toward inspiring individuals and persuading them to give it their best. Tracy Brower expands on this concept:

> All the leadership literature says that culture is a mirror of the leader. If you don't have passion, people are brilliant at picking that up, and you cannot fake it for long. If you don't have the passion, your employees will not be passionate about what they do. Maybe you'll get compliance, but you are not going to have people who wake up and can't wait to go work. Everybody has the instinct to matter. If you aren't creating that sense of energy and purpose, you will have retention issues.[4]

That is especially true when there are difficult times. For example, when you need people to take on additional responsibilities without additional pay, or work with a demanding customer. Having passion helps you persevere when the going gets tough. This was never more evident than during the COVID-19 pandemic. Business owners did everything they could to continue to work despite government shutdowns, regulations, and lack of workers. They are doing the same to this day.

Passion also impacts the businessperson's interactions with customers and suppliers. People do business with people. That is a well-known fact. It is much easier to persuade someone to buy from you when you spend time with them, work harder to bring them great products or ideas, and let them see firsthand your passion for what you do.

Evolving Your Passion

The one thing that I have noticed over the years is that *what* I am passionate about has changed. When I opened the doors, I was excited about launching our services. The first sale and signing that first big contract were overwhelming. I was thrilled that someone believed in what we were doing. As time went on, I was passionate about the new technologies we invested in. I was always looking to learn about new ways of doing business. I was excited to network with other entrepreneurs and discover how they navigated the same challenges I faced.

Today, I am enthusiastic about quite different things. While I still love competing for a new client's business and creating something that works for them, I am more passionate about my team. I love helping them grow personally and professionally. I don't need to be out front. I enjoy watching and coaching them through the work. I love seeing the passion they have for serving our customers. I delight in the fact that they are "all in" when it comes to the business.

The reality is that no one can be consistently upbeat and passionate. At every phase of your business, there are times when passion ebbs and flows. Having a team that shares your passion is critical if you want to have staying power. The energy they bring to the business takes some of the burden off the owner. That's why it is critical to hire the right people at the right time. We will talk more about that in chapter 6. You also need to be sure that you don't fall into the trap of believing that what you are creating will last forever. Actress Lauren Bacall said, "Standing still is the fastest way of moving backwards in a rapidly changing world."

And this is a world where change is more rapid than ever before. How many of us are hampered because we resist change and instead just do what we have always done? Let's face it, we get comfortable in our roles and are sometimes on autopilot. We believe that we know the business and have perfected the processes and procedures. Maybe we think that the product or service can't be improved. Having passion at the outset of your business is easy. Keeping the passion alive and having the staying power to succeed long term is not.

Take Time Out. Rejuvenate Your Passion.

If you find yourself overburdened in the early years of the business, that is completely normal—take a time-out. This is easier said than done for small-business owners. We believe, rightly or wrongly, that we need to be present. We don't. In fact, taking off a few days or even a few hours can make you feel like a kid who is skipping school. It feels great. It gives your staff a chance to step up, and the break helps you rejuvenate your passion.

You can also take time out to learn something new, take a class, or attend a workshop. You may just be feeling a little bored and need to get the creative juices flowing. One thing that always energizes me is talking to other business owners. That is something that Edward Lowe, the inventor of Kitty Litter, missed out on. It is said that he launched more than just a product. He founded a whole new industry. Ed was an entrepreneur; it was in his DNA. He had 32 patents, 115 trademarks, and 36 copyrights. Most of us start one or two businesses. Ed owned some seventy businesses. He had passion for business and as a part of his legacy wanted to help other entrepreneurs so they would not be alone on their journey. In 1985, he and his wife, Darlene, founded the Edward Lowe Foundation, an operating organization focused on second-stage businesses, which sits on two thousand acres of woodlands, prairies, ponds, and streams.

The Edward Lowe Foundation offers leadership retreats to help second-stage business owners step away from the day-to-day demands of the business and talk with like-minded people about both business and personal issues. You might not recognize it, but sometimes you just need to hit the "pause button." Colleen Killen-Roberts, VP of entrepreneurship, says:

> We believe that entrepreneurs have the answers. We just create the space to help them get there. We have this beautiful piece of property that they can use in the way that Mr. Lowe did—for pondering, creating that buffer away from their life. Entrepreneurs know what they're passionate about better than anyone else. We challenge

them to ask, "What makes you happy? What makes you tick? What are you doing when you feel the most alive?" We put them together with other entrepreneurs. Entrepreneurs by themselves are powerful, but entrepreneurs with their peers are magical. They start to talk about challenges. They brainstorm and share ideas. And in that environment, they get back to that creative feeling they had when they started the business.[5]

Change Your Scenery. Reignite Your Passion.

Sometimes a change of scenery can reignite your passion. Around 2008, I purchased a building for my business. It was a terrific location, near an expressway that made it easy to get to several of our large customers. We remodeled the entire building, and it was a great space. Until it wasn't. Our customer base changed. We often headed to the airport across town in major traffic. Our once cool space got old and tired.

In 2022, we sold that building and relocated. While this might seem trivial, it has had a profound impact on morale. The staff played an integral role in choosing the new location and designing the space. A new space that is fresh, clean, and updated helps you think differently about work. It also gives you a chance to rethink your environment. Is it working well for you?

Over the years, studies by architectural firms and furniture manufacturers have shown that the physical environment has a significant impact on business success. Businesses with great environments generally have higher profits, better employee engagement, and a stronger brand. And it just feels good going to a nice new office. Can location also impact your passion for work? Yes. For me moving my office closer to home and the airport has taken the stress out of the commute. When I get to work, I am ready to work. Employees report they are also less stressed, and we have other businesses in this new location—happy hour is now a regular occurrence with the neighbors. The change of scenery has resulted in a change of attitude, for everyone.

I believe that the happiest and most successful business owners have a great deal of passion for their work, their employees, and their customers. Barbara Corcoran said it best, "You can't fake passion. I've learned to look for the same three qualities in every business owner: passion, high energy, and thankfulness." So, ask yourself, do you have the passion, and can you sustain that passion?

TIPS TO SUCCEED

- ▸ Make a list of what excites you about your business.
- ▸ Commit the time that it will take to be successful.
- ▸ Write down your definition of business success and read it every day.
- ▸ Be realistic about the challenges to achieving success.

4

GET SMART ABOUT PARTNERING: CREATE A BUSINESS PRENUP

Growing up in a family-owned business, I witnessed the importance of what I call a "business prenup." Take the time to understand what each partner brings to the table and how the partnership will work. Without doing this, a "divorce," can be painful—financially and emotionally.

When entrepreneurs go into business, they often struggle with this dilemma: partner up or buy the talent you need to get started. Many do what I did and make the leap with a partner. Some might wonder why I thought I needed a partner. Actually, there were many times over the course of the partnership when I asked myself, "What were you thinking?" I could say I wasn't thinking, but that would not be honest. My business is a media-production and communications consulting company. It has some very definite areas of expertise; there is the creative part and the technical side. I have always been good at the creative aspect, and I have technical ability as well. But I did not think that I had enough expertise to handle all the changes in technology that are so much a part of this business. That's why I decided to partner up; I thought it would be a good blend of talents. I chose someone whom I worked with at a TV station. We started freelancing together, and it worked well. When I decided to open the business, it seemed like a logical move.

At the time, I thought I knew him fairly well, but we did not have the kind of conversations that I now know are critical to any business relationship. The truth is, you never really know how someone will react in a business setting until you are there together, working down in the trenches.

How a Business Prenup Differs from the Traditional Prenup

Many people today go into a marriage with a prenuptial agreement. Why? Because they know there are always negative things that can happen, and they want to protect themselves. Prenuptial agreements vary widely, but they usually include provisions for support: how you will divide property, grounds for forfeiture of assets, and so on.

When you have a partner, you need to properly define the business issues: structure, percent of ownership, buy-out conditions, etc. This needs to be done exceedingly early in the process of starting a business. It is tricky and delicate, as delicate as asking your fiancé for a prenuptial agreement. Does it mean you think the venture will fail? Do you not trust your partner? Or are you simply being realistic?

Of course, there are the typical areas to address. What if someone wants out? What if one partner is no longer able to work for health reasons? How will you evaluate the worth of the business? What happens in the case of bankruptcy? But there are other personal issues that you need to address that are not usually part of a legal agreement. These are the fuzzy, gray areas that pop up because everyone has their own unique personality, style of working, and values. This is where my concept of the business prenup goes beyond the typical things you think of with traditional agreements.

Get Personal and Ask Questions

When developing a business prenup, you need to set aside time to ask each other a number of questions. This is not a single conversation but a series of conversations. Take notes; then you can go back and refer to them later to see if they resonate after the discussion. Here are some of the areas to address:

- What do you know about the person's family, background, and values? They say that business is business, but it's also personal, and that is influenced greatly by family.

- Do you have personalities that complement each other?

- Do you want to spend time with this person? You will see them more than you see your own family.

- Do either of you have problems with anger, such as passive/aggressive behavior? No one is likely to tell you this, so you have to be observant. This is one that can cost you big customers, issues with employees, and legal bills when things get out of hand.

- Will a spouse or significant other be involved in the business? If so, who calls the shots?

- What is your idea of work/life balance? Does it match your partner's perspective?

- Does anything about the person bother you? Do they talk too much? Do they seem too controlling? Are they too easygoing?

- Do they socialize with people that make you uncomfortable? Do they engage in risky behavior?

- Have they ever been in trouble, even as a child (which won't be on their record)?

- Are they good communicators? This is one point that many people discount yet is one of the most important. If your partner does not communicate with you frequently and effectively, you will find yourself in the middle of situations you did not anticipate. Then you end up in a reactive mode, instead of a proactive one.

- Do they pay attention to their health and wellness? Is their lifestyle a healthy one?

- Do they coast through situations, avoiding confrontation?

- Do they tell lies (even little white ones) or exaggerate the truth?

- Do they have a positive outlook, or are they more focused on the negative?

- ▸ Are they solution-oriented or problem-oriented?

- ▸ Do they have a sense of humor? Are they able to laugh at themselves and not take themselves too seriously?

- ▸ Do they make excuses for things that go wrong or take responsibility?

- ▸ Are they willing to ask for help?

That last question is very important. When you are a small-business owner, you simply can't know it all. You must rely on trusted advisors, peers, and others to help you navigate difficult situations. If you can't ask for help, you are doomed to make mistakes. Watch carefully to see if your potential partner is a know-it-all or has developed the habit of reaching out for assistance.

Ask Business-Related Questions

Once you have gotten through all the personal prenup questions, it is time to get down to more specifically business-related points:

- ▸ How big do you want to grow the business?

- ▸ What kind of customers do you want to connect with and win? If your partner is afraid of big businesses, and some are, you will not be able to capture that market.

- ▸ How will you make hiring decisions? What if you don't agree about whether to hire or who to hire?

- ▸ How much financial risk are you comfortable with?

- ▸ Who will be your outside resources and what will they do? Some business owners insist on doing activities that are better left to outside resources. If you end up with a partner that is a "do-it-yourselfer," it can get you in real trouble. This is especially important when it comes to the legal and accounting areas. Laws and requirements change all the time. If you don't have professionals to help keep you up to date, you may find yourself paying fines or worse.

- ▸ What will be a typical workweek? This can cause issues if one person feels like they are putting more time into the business than the other.

- How much money should be reinvested in the business?
- How will you decide on salary adjustments? Will you both be paid equally, or should you get paid on the value of the work? Is one type of work more important than another?
- What will you do when you disagree?
- How will you reward employees?
- Until what age do you want to work?
- How much will you donate to charity, and how will you decide who to support?

Throughout the years that I had a partner, each and every one of these questions caused an issue. Sometimes it was a minor conversation, other times it was a huge fight. As I mentioned earlier, at one point, we even went to business counseling. The situation that brought it to a head was the decision to hire an additional person so that we could take on more work. My partner did not want to let go of some of his responsibilities. In fact, he did not want to share his knowledge with our employees so that they could take on more responsibility, freeing us up to do higher-level work. He wanted control of every aspect of the business. This meant that we simply could not continue to grow. It became obvious to me that our vision for the business did not match. In truth, I knew that there would be differences of opinion, but I never thought it would reach the point where one of us had to leave.

As it worked out, I stayed, and he went. That opened up a whole new avenue for the business. I made many adjustments, hired people, invested in equipment, and sought out new customers. It took a while, but all of these efforts have made the business even more successful.

A Final Thought

The decision to partner up is one that can bring you great joy and security or can lead to huge issues. I think back on my decision to partner up and believe I should have paid much more attention to the business prenup. I should have asked the questions, then really listened and observed to see if the answers added up. Sometimes we hear what we want to hear—that is exactly what I did. I did not pay attention to the personal and business prenup. I should have been smarter about partnering up. The buy-sell agreement did make it easier to get out, but if I had paid more attention to the list of questions, I wouldn't have started the business with that partner. I would have gone it alone or found someone more suitable. Today I know that I could have made it alone because I do have the skill set needed and can get the talent to fill in the gaps, as I have done since my "business divorce."

TIPS TO SUCCEED

▸ If you are thinking about partnering up, set aside time to ask both business and personal questions.

▸ Take notes or record the conversation so that you can both review it later.

▸ Consider getting outside assistance to facilitate the discussion before you partner up.

▸ Revisit the business prenup every few years. You need to be prepared because things change, and people change.

▸ Don't be afraid to go it alone and hire the skill set you need.

5
SHOW ME
THE MONEY

One of the biggest issues that every entrepreneur faces is taking a great idea or product and turning it into a viable business. The issue is M-O-N-E-Y. The statistics are grim. Over the years, small businesses have faced serious problems getting loans, and it is still true today. According to the National Small Business Association (NSBA) Economic Survey Report: "One of the most concerning trends throughout the data is clear tightening of lending. Today, more than one-third of small businesses (37 percent) say they are unable to obtain adequate financing—the highest this indicator has been since 2008, the start of the housing market collapse which kicked-off the great recession." The report goes on to note that "the number of small businesses who said they are unable to grow or expand their business operations due to a lack of capital is at its highest point since 2007."[1]

Sandy Jelinski is the CEO and president of Lake Michigan Credit Union, the sixteenth-largest credit union in the nation. When asked about the challenges that small businesses face today in term of loans, Jelinski said:

> Today, a lot of the larger financial institutions are focusing their efforts on larger, more profitable loans. In some cases, it takes just as much time to review the qualifications for a fifteen-million-dollar loan as it does for a $500,000 loan, so instead of thirty small loans, they can focus on one large loan. It often comes down to looking for efficiencies, but this makes it much harder for a small business . . . often their loan isn't even considered because they don't meet a minimum size requirement. Small businesses are also often considered

more risky because of more limited capital and operating size, so they get turned away.[2]

Small-business owners confirm this is a challenge. But at the same time, we are constantly being bombarded by ads about how quickly loans can be obtained. We hear stories about "angel investors" who are looking for opportunities to hand out cash. It is confusing. Marilyn D. Landis, president of Basic Business Concepts, Inc., explains it this way, "There's too much money and it's the wrong kind, given to the wrong people at the wrong time."[3] We will discuss this in greater detail later, but first let's go deeper into the broader financial issues facing small-business owners.

Volatility. Margins. Debt.

One might say that there is always some volatility, but this is a time of intense volatility in business markets. Customer needs and preferences are changing. Products are changing to meet those needs. The supply chain is experiencing continued chaos after the COVID pandemic. Some believe it will take years to return to the stable prepandemic supply chains. All of this is having a financial impact on those starting or trying to grow a business. Landis says:

> We must learn how to manage through volatility and chaos. In the past, things were very predictable and linear. That is no longer true. Some of us grew up in a chaotic time, but we have a generation who did not. We have to teach them how to manage their finances through chaos.[4]

That is exactly what Landis and other experienced business advisors are doing. Unlike the days when advisors retired at sixty-five, these individuals are finding that younger entrepreneurs are among their fastest growing and most committed clients. This younger generation is tech savvy and energetic. However, they may not know where the "potholes" are in the market. Their older advisors do know and are helping them manage through the chaos. Suddenly, those of us who have been in business for decades are cool again to this younger generation. They are seeking out older advisors, networking with them, and attending the same business conferences.

Another area that needs attention is tight margins. As businesses face increasing costs, many are unable to get the margins they need. Here, too, Landis says there is a lack of understanding.

> We haven't taught anyone how to measure volume in decades. We talk to clients about gross profit margin. They often can't get their margin anymore for a lot of reasons, and it is unpredictable, too. They may have the margin set. Then they land a big contract, but the steel—or some other material—went up 20 percent. So at my company, we teach clients about volume. That is much harder to measure, but if they have the right volume coming through the business, they can survive on the lower margins.[5]

Throughout my years as a business owner, I have been vigilant about not carrying too much debt. How much is too much? That varies but without capital, small businesses cannot achieve their goals. Think about it. You can't launch a business or new initiative. You can't expand. You don't even dare to think about hiring more employees and might need to lay employees off. You don't have the money to market your product or services. You might not be able to buy or lease the new equipment you need to meet the requirements of new sales efforts. Not to mention, you must purchase inventory to meet the demand. And if customers take ninety days to pay, which many do, it affects your cash flow.

You might be tempted to go for that big loan, but be careful. You want to stay nimble. That means you need the "right" funding. Marilyn Landis explains that traditional financing may not be the best option today.

> It is too easy to get a loan secured by real estate. You own a building, and the bank says, "Great, you own a building, we can make you a loan." As you go forward, that real estate may no longer have the value it once had. Or perhaps you get to a point where you don't need the building; now you are stuck.[6]

The Need for Funding

So how big is the need for funding? I asked Sandy Jelinski, CEO and president of Lake Michigan Credit Union, to describe the current situation.

Jelinski said, "The SBA loan market size is thirty billion dollars a year, which tells me there is a great need for affordable loans to help fuel the growth of the over thirty-three million small business in the US, of which tens of thousands are in our market areas."[7]

Most people have a personal relationship with a bank or credit union. In the search to fund their business, that is where they start. But how do you know what is your best option? Should you have several financial relationships? There are differing opinions. I believe you need to fully explore the possibilities. Marilyn Landis offers this advice:

> A good way to test your bank is to call your longtime banker and say, "There is an opportunity in a new market. I'm looking at investing in this new market, a new product, or hiring additional people. Can you help me with the loan?" There are a few lenders out there who remember and are back to doing projection lending. Ninety-eight percent of them right now are not there. If the bank says, "I don't know if we can do that"; if a bank can't be flexible, you need to know that. I have a client who had been with his bank for twenty-six years. They turned on him. He did not leave soon enough.[8]

Over the years, I have been fortunate when seeking funding, but those who need loans today may have a very different experience. Here is the reality. The owner impacts the financial situation of a small business. That is because the owner is, in many cases, the business. If something happens to the owner, the business is at risk. And if the owner has something negative on their FICO score, banks will not make the loan.

Banks are also consolidating. The bank you work with may now be part of a bigger bank that has a different lending formula that puts smaller businesses at a disadvantage. The opposite may also be true. The bigger banks might have more capacity and a greater emphasis on small business. Many believe that banking regulators need to find a different and better way of evaluating small business. Perhaps the FICO score is not the answer to handing out loans. That is one solution offered by the National Small Business Association (NSBA), along with the idea that "regulators should seek to ease restrictions on lenders for smaller loans since a one-size-fits-all formula doesn't often work for many small businesses and start-ups."

When I started my business, I researched a Small Business Administration loan. The process, for me, was time-consuming and frustrating. The paperwork alone was unbelievable, especially when you consider the fact that I wasn't looking for a huge amount of money—less than $80,000. I found another option. For some small businesses, an SBA loan might be the only way they can get approved. But even today, many complain that the process is complicated and needs to be streamlined.

According to the NSBA's 2023–2024 Issue Brief, "In FY 2022, SBA guaranteed nearly 47,700 7(a) loans worth $25.7 billion to small businesses. Unfortunately, SBA has time and again found itself a political football with lawmakers failing to promptly reauthorize funding levels and give the agency the flexibility needed to ensure all small businesses have access to financing."[9]

Credit unions are gaining in popularity because they can help fill the credit gap. Unlike banks, they are not-for-profit and are driven by their members. They often charge lower fees on business accounts and have lower loan rates. Credit unions also service a business owner's individual mortgage, checking, savings, credit cards, and auto loan needs, plus those of their employees. For example, Lake Michigan Credit Union's philosophy has been to consistently do what is right for their members, which has fueled their growth. While satisfaction rates for big banks have been declining, credit unions like LMCU often get high marks. Sandy Jelinski offers this explanation:

> I believe credit unions, by their very nature, have very strong local community focus and are very committed and open to helping small, local businesses succeed. Ninety-nine point nine percent of all businesses are small businesses, defined as having under five hundred employees by the SBA, and almost 50 percent of all employees in the US are employed by small businesses. Credit unions actively target small businesses for growth, unlike a lot of the larger financial institutions [FIs]. Plus, with credit unions, there is local decision-making and a strong desire to create a relationship. Often, larger FIs, if they will consider a small-business prospect, require more paperwork and out-of-market decision-making, which may not take local market factors into consideration. We

love working with all of our business members, and we find it very rewarding to be able to service their individual mortgage, checking, savings, credit cards, and auto loans needs, plus those of their employees.[10]

However, credit unions have limitations. The NSBA notes, "They can only lend 12.25 percent of the worth of their assets to businesses—leaving billions of dollars of potential loans to businesses off the table."[11] Still according to Jelinski, there are many reasons to consider a credit union. Jelinski says:

LMCU has a very strong balance sheet and extensive commercial lending division, which includes a SBA division focused on helping small businesses. We need to maintain a strong capital ratio, which we have. A current challenge, facing banks and credit unions, is the rising rate environment and the need to grow deposits to fund loans. A lot of consumers are using their savings to pay down debt, which reduces, to some degree, the available capital to lend. When it comes to small-business loans, they typically fall in the $500,000 to five-million-dollar range. A part of the SBA loan is guaranteed by the federal government, so the US government assumes some of the risk, which makes it easier to lend to a smaller company. As long as the business has positive cash flow, a reasonable loan request, and a strong business plan and the ability to service their debt, they are strong candidates for a loan.[12]

Alternative Lending

Marilyn Landis knows a lot about alternative lending. That's because as a former commercial lender, she was exposed to hundreds of entrepreneurs who were talented at developing their product or service but typically lacked the financial expertise needed to run a company. Landis worked for three of the largest SBA lenders in the country. During her career, she has secured financing for income properties, construction projects, manufacturers, restaurants and hotels—handling everything from microloans to $22,000,000 fundings.

When Landis launched her business back in 2001, she believed that smart entrepreneurs could position themselves to do more than just survive—they could thrive if they had the needed access to affordable CFO-level skills that were customized to each business. Essentially, her company acts as the CFO in the C-suite for small businesses. Landis says that individuals try to put the alternate lending market into one bucket, but it is very diverse, from economic development agencies to high-net-worth individuals who are direct lenders or investors. The trick is to know where you fit and understand the implications. Landis says:

> There are economic development agencies who are willing to give you all this great money at great terms, but they still have to get paid back. It's well intended. Often I tell a start-up, if they're lending money for the wrong thing, how are you going to pay it back? For years, everybody was told, get as much money as you can. It's cheap money, three- and three-quarter percent for thirty years. Now suddenly they may have a million-dollar debt on the balance sheet. They have a monthly payment over the next thirty years. And you don't stiff the government or take a short payoff with the government. We have people paying off loans into their retirement years.[13]

One thing to note, no matter what type of funding you seek in the alternative market, you have to do your homework to find reputable sources, because this is an unregulated part of the financial market. Landis says you should find out what others' experience has been with these lenders because "you might discover that your angel is really a devil."[14]

Angel or Devil

As my search for the money to launch the company continued, I was approached by a successful businessperson who heard about my venture and offered to invest. Of course, he wanted a good-sized piece of the business. Think *Shark Tank*, that popular TV show where entrepreneurs try to get the celebrity panel to invest. Some of the contestants trade a significant piece of their business for cash. Others walk away. That's what I did. I walked away and continued the search.

This businessperson, by today's definition, would be an "angel investor." An angel investor is generally an affluent individual who provides backing for a business start-up, usually in exchange for convertible debt or ownership equity. There are also angel groups or angel networks available. These are individuals who get together and pool their dollars and then invest in business opportunities. This lets them share research on the companies and theoretically spreads out the risk to all the investors.

A lot of people think that angel investors are the way to go. But some experts I spoke with warn that the vast majority of small businesses have *no business* looking for an angel investor. That's because they cannot pay the kind of returns an angel investor will demand. Of course, there are always exceptions.

Some individuals get creative and use crowdfunding to get the money they need. One thing to note is that there are some complex regulations here, so use caution. Others turn to a private loan from family or friends. For decades, it was an unwritten rule: don't borrow money from family or friends. But, in truth, this is how many small businesses have gotten their start over the years. And, as credit has gotten tighter, family and friends are stepping up even more. My advice here is simple. Even with family and friends, don't take shortcuts. Have a legal document that spells out how much money is on the table and how it will be repaid.

Predatory Lenders

There is no lack of slick ads and online offers for funding. Imagine this: It is late at night, and you are worrying about how to fund your next big project or growth initiative. You get an email. With the click of a button, you can get the money you need instantly. But at what cost? Many charge outrageous fees, and these predatory lenders use tactics that work. Landis says she has seen it many times.

> You are growing, and your cash flow is at its worst. You get this email, and you click. Then you find out that they're going to hit your checking account, and it is 35 percent. You're struggling, but you manage to pay down a little bit. Then in the middle of the night, they say, "We will lower your rate if you refinance and add more money." It is like the gambler that thinks if they play one more hand, it will pay off what they have lost.[15]

Landis admittedly prefers alternative lending to traditional sources for a variety of reasons, but she offers a few words of warning, "I work with my clients and tell them it is like credit cards. If you live on your credit cards, it's going to kill you. You have got to know when to get in and when to get out. You have to have a strategy."[16]

I would add these words of caution. Entrepreneurs are dreamers. They are builders. They are just plain excited about their idea or business. What they often forget to consider is the risk that the bank, the credit union, or any other lender is taking. If you are consistently getting turned down by credible sources, there is probably a good reason. Do not be insulted. Maybe you have not done the work to prepare for what might happen if things go terribly wrong. Or your contingency plans are not credible. Perhaps you should listen to what your advisors are saying and get educated.

Know Your Numbers

How you manage money and your credit is one of the most critical aspects of business. In one final piece of advice, Landis says to check out the Risk Management Association (RMA) averages. You can get a subscription for service or find it at a business library. This tells you essential information by the North American Industry Classification System (NAICS) code. Things such as average profit margins, what percentage the employer gets paid, what the employees get paid, how many days it takes to get paid on their receivables, payables, leverage ratios, and much more. It is historic information divided by company size and by asset size.

Knowing how you stack up is critical, according to Landis. She says, "What you have to do is take that responsibility on yourself. The alternative market won't discipline you. Banks won't discipline you. You must discipline yourself. Good financials, good control of borrowing, don't over-borrow, don't over-leverage."[17]

TIPS TO SUCCEED

▸ There are a number of different options for accessing capital and you should understand your needs at a specific point in time to find the best source.

- ▸ Do your homework. Check out your lender. What have others experienced when working with them? In this age of the internet, go digging to find independent comments.

- ▸ If you use alternative lending, get in and get out quickly.

- ▸ If lots of lenders say "no," there is a reason. Perhaps you should listen.

6

HIRE THE RIGHT PEOPLE AT THE RIGHT TIME

L ong hours. Nonexistent weekends. No personal time. New business owners expect that they will spend most of their waking hours working, and they certainly can if they want to. Every entrepreneur knows that it takes a lot of sacrifice to build a business, especially if you are going after big customers that have big needs. Call us crazy, but we thrive on getting the work done—no matter how many hours we have to spend.

There are, however, some business consultants and owners that I think are bordering on delusional. I don't understand those who say you can work a four-hour workweek. I think not. I know a few who believe you should only answer your emails or pick up voice mails once a day so you can be more productive. And others say you don't need to have your cell phone on 24/7. Just try explaining to your customer why you didn't respond to a call for help when they had an issue at 9:00 p.m. on a Friday night. Believe me; this happens, especially with large customers who consider you to be part of their extended staff.

It takes a huge effort to run a great small business. And, when you start to attract larger customers, the effort can become herculean. Even I, a steadfast do-it-yourselfer, had to ask, "When is the right time to bring on some help?"

When Is the Right Time to Hire?

Many business owners struggle with the decision to hire. They often procrastinate because they are afraid to make a commitment when there is uncertainty about new legislation, taxes, and the like. Hiring is, indeed, an art in itself. There are consultants and tools to help. There are personality tests such as Myers-Briggs and DiSC Assessments—even Dr. Phil has one. These tests can help reveal aspects of a person's character or psychological makeup. I have used some of these tools and even a consultant or two. But ultimately, it's about knowing the right time to hire, and then finding the right people. So how do you do that? Let's start with when to hire.

I think there are milestones, conditions, and events that trigger this decision. The most obvious one is that you simply cannot get the work done, or the product out the door, in a timely manner. You notice that you don't have the time to communicate with your customers. They are calling you to ask when projects will be done or product delivered. Let's face it, you are underwater. Is it the right time to hire? Will the surge of business continue? Perhaps this is just a seasonal bump in business or due to unexpected conditions, like a storm that causes lots of damage so that construction workers are in demand.

This is when having a little historical perspective can help. If you know that the bump in business is because customers are trying to get year-end projects done, you can plan for it. Too often, businesses make knee-jerk decisions; this is the downfall of well-laid plans. You need to be disciplined, or you just might jump and hire someone for all the wrong reasons. Look at your internal operations and understand the ebbs and flows of the business cycles or seasons. I keep track of my big customers' corporate year-ends. Why? Because many of them have budgets they need to spend down, last-minute projects that come up, or work that needs to be completed to meet some plan. These big surges of work can put a strain on a business.

But there may be other reasons you can't get the work done. Perhaps your employees are just not very productive or don't have the right tools in place to get the job done efficiently. A business owner told me that she had to fire an employee for inappropriate conduct. She was very worried because they were going into a busy season, so she took the former employee's work and redistributed it to the remaining workers. She thought this would solve the problem until they could hire a replacement, but a funny thing happened: the work was getting done faster and better than in the past. The employer discovered, much to her dismay, that the former employee was not very productive and that she was spending a lot of time surfing the internet and shopping online! The business owner did not need to hire another person after all.

Having the right tools is also critical. At my office, we have eight video editing systems. Years ago, each one was a stand-alone system. Trying to balance the work was a nightmare. We would load up the video for a project on one system only to discover that something else on the drives was suddenly needed by a customer. That brought work on one project to a standstill. That is not very productive when it happens on a regular basis. The answer was to put the proper tools in place—shared computer video storage. Now, any project can be accessed on any system. There is a lot less waiting around and a lot greater productivity. Giving people the right tools may help save you from having to staff up for big projects.

Look to Fill the Gaps

My business recently had a huge surge in the number of projects we were handling. One week, I had three crews in four states. Yes, I know that sounds funny, but one crew visited two states. I started to think we needed to add a person. When I asked my staff, I was surprised to find that they didn't want me to hire. Why? They wanted to work more hours during the business spikes and earn more bonus money. That's okay, but the truth is that sometimes you need to really beef up your staff and be proactive. Look at the skill set of your current employees. Is there a gap? If you want to bring in new accounts or launch new revenue streams, do you have the talent to do that? Remember, new customers require extra time in the initial phase of doing business, so you will need backup.

If you add services or new products, you need individuals who have the skills to do the work or sell. You may not have that capability with your current staff, and it might take way too much time to get them trained. As many of our corporate clients eliminated staff or restructured, we were being asked to take on tasks that were a stretch; for example, graphic design of digital and print materials to accompany videos. This included things like lesson templates, infographics, and illustrations. While we had never pre-viously hired a graphic designer in-house, it became obvious that there was a critical need for that expertise. We began by reaching out to a university and hired an intern. It went so well that we hired a person full time. That has expanded what we can offer and made our video production more efficient and creative.

Another gap may occur when you expand your geographic reach; you might need people to cover those areas. Yes, technology has made it easier to work across the miles, but there are times when you need to be where your customers are to meet tight timelines or provide responsive service. If your employees are telling you that they are overwhelmed, and you know they are productive and have the right tools, then it's probably time to hire. The biggest reason to hire new talent is to help you have the time to focus on the business, especially if you want to grow, attract big customers, or change direction.

Setting Up an Employee to Succeed or Fail

Timing is everything. Bring in a new person too early, and you may not have enough to keep them busy; they get bored and leave. Bring in a new person too late, and they may be overwhelmed by the amount of work that needs to be done. If you have to err on one side or the other, go for too early.

Sometimes, we set up an employee to fail. That's because we bring them in when we are completely overwhelmed. The people who should be training them have no time. Small-business owners are notorious for thinking employ-ees will magically get it and become assimilated into their organization. They might receive basic orientation—how to use email, the phone system, where to find things, etc.—but they are not getting what they really need: proper and strategic onboarding. That's much different from a simple orientation.

Onboarding Can Create Employee Superstars

When you run a small business, so much knowledge of your company (such as its mission, how it works) is in your head, not on paper. I am not saying that is good, but it is usually the case. You need to write all that information down and share it if you want employees to be superstars. When it comes to the business, they need to know:

- Company history
- Mission—the task that it is every employee's duty to carry out
- Values—what is important and what you believe in
- Vision—where the company is going
- How do customers view the company, products, and services? Who are your big customers?
- What are the biggest opportunities and challenges?

The cultural aspects of the business are just as important as, if not more important than, all the business information. I say that because small companies are often tightly knit. You can't go and hide somewhere to avoid your fellow workers. When it comes to the company culture, employees need to know:

- How do you make decisions? Is this a collaborative effort? Is the business owner the sole decision-maker?
- What is the personality of the company? Usually, in a small company, it mirrors the owner's personality.
- Are there rules that everyone knows but are not written?

The Right Person for a Small Business

So now that you have determined that you need to hire and you have thought about the process of onboarding, is there a right person for your organization? Yes! And here's a really important thing to know: the right person for a small business looks very different from the right person for a big business. Many job seekers are interested in companies with recognizable names or prestigious addresses. They are really excited about titles. The longer and more impressive sounding, the better. They need defined job descriptions, and they want the perks that come with a larger organization. These are individuals that probably won't do well in a smaller company where it is all hands on deck. In a small company, employees may walk into something new and different every day. They need to be comfortable with uncertainty and actually get a rush out of the unexpected things that may happen every day.

I made a huge mistake with an individual that I thought would be the right person for our company. She worked at a large retailer in the marketing department. In her position, she was responsible for a variety of different types of communications. She decided that she wanted to make a move to a smaller company where she thought she would be a better fit. In fact, she sold me on how excited she was to work in a setting where she could be more hands-on with projects. It did not take long for me and the rest of the staff to figure out that the fit was miserable.

She believed she had the skills to do the job and spoke articulately about managing the job requirements. The problem was that she did not realize how little she actually did at her former job. There were lots of people to support her, and much of the real work was being done by those around her. She was directing the work, not doing it. When she tried to do the work for us, it did not meet our standards. It all came to a head when a big client called and told me never to send her out again because she simply did not know what she was doing. I tried to coach her, but she was not the right person. She was a better fit for a big company.

When you do not find the right people, you are putting yourself at risk. Clients who know your company come to expect a certain type of person as an employee. When someone does not meet their expectations, they start to question how good you really are and if they should be working with you.

You might wonder, "How long do you wait before terminating someone that just does not measure up?" I have a ninety-day probation period. Some companies have less, some more. I can usually tell within the first ninety days if someone has the potential to be a good fit, but even I have been fooled. Some people are on their best behavior until they are off probation, and then you see a very different individual than the one you hired. One thing I can tell you, the really great employees shine, and you know it immediately. The really terrible ones are also easy to spot. It is those who fall in the middle that test your ability as a manager. Pay close attention to these individuals.

Think about New Ways to Recruit

How do you find the right person? Traditional methods of recruitment, such as placing ads and using temporary employees, may work for some but may not be the best options. I've tried wading through piles of resumés and conducting marathon interviews. It can be time-consuming and often fruitless. I tried a staffing company; they posted the job and did the initial interviews but did not turn up great prospects. In fairness, maybe we did not communicate our needs and wants effectively to them. Or maybe we just didn't use the right search firm. You need to look for the right people in the right places.

One thing to consider is finding college or university programs that require their students to do internships. We have such a relationship with a college that has seniors do a six-month internship. It has been a great way to get a feel for the individual's capabilities and fit with our organization. We have hired a number of them upon graduation.

Some of my best hires have come from extremely targeted efforts. The last time I needed a project manager, I did not place ads. I wrote one, but then used my connections on LinkedIn to spread the word. I was clear with my contacts. I asked them to only send me individuals that met the requirements and that they believed would be a good fit with our company's culture. Because these people knew us or had worked with us, they got it. The response was amazing. I interviewed at least three individuals that could do the job and would fit in with our culture. It was just a matter of a few weeks, and we made an offer.

Think about it: no expense, no ads, no wading through countless resumés of people who did not even meet the basic requirements. Now it doesn't always work, but when it does, it makes hiring easy. For this kind of personal and targeted effort to work, you must be extremely well networked with your online community and within the professional circles that are key to your industry. Otherwise, you will not get a great response when you reach out for help.

Don't Focus on Specific Skills: Think Bigger

Let's say you get excellent referrals. Now how do you make sure the individual is the right person for a position? I find that employers always have

55

a list of skills that are needed for the job and fairly well-defined experience requirements in terms of years or capabilities. I have found a better way. I don't just look for specific skills, because I think you can teach skills. I believe you can't teach the kinds of things that really make an individual successful and that can help your business as you try to connect with and win big business. You won't know if you have the right person until they start working for you. But here are a few things to consider when looking at a candidate.

- **Creativity:** Does the individual look at the job with fresh eyes? Can they see ways to influence the process, the product, the others around them? Do you think they have the ability to inspire others to think in new and different ways?

- **Motivation:** Does the individual really love what they are doing? I often ask this question: "If you weren't doing this, what would you love to do most?" If they have something they want to do more than the job you are offering, then walk away. Are they motivated to keep learning? Do they take the initiative to stay up to date on things like software, equipment that you might need, and trends in the business? My staff has turned thumbs down on candidates because they did not believe that they would be a good fit, work as hard as the rest of the team, or have the right attitude about serving our customers.

- **Problem-solving:** Some individuals want you to tell them what to do and how to do it. Business moves too fast to hold someone's hand or direct every move, even at entry-level jobs. We need employees who can solve problems and think on their own. Of course, this means you will have to accept the fact that they might not solve it the way you do. But as long as the job gets done with great results, that is what is important. This is especially critical to your business when there are few hands on deck with a lot to accomplish.

- **Communication:** The ability to communicate is also high on my list. We have washed out a number of skilled applicants because they simply could not carry on a conversation. Maybe this is the result of too much tweeting and texting. Communication is a broad area; we stress verbal, nonverbal, writing, video conferencing skills, and much more. When you work with larger customers, who may or may not be geographically close, you need to be an expert at communication.

▶ **Attitude:** While the right skill set is important, the right attitude—a willingness to work hard and learn—is the most important trait I look for in a new employee. I look for individuals who are "all in." They will do whatever it takes to get the job and keep it. I've seen job seekers boldly walk into an interview with their list of wants. They want a regular schedule. One individual told me he needed to be home on Tuesdays and Thursdays in time for his wife to go to yoga. I promptly told him I routinely cancel my Pilates session because a customer needs me. They don't want to travel. They want higher starting pay. I don't always expect to find the perfect fit with a new employee in terms of skill level and experience. I do want someone who really wants to work and has a passion for the job.

Get Employees Involved in Hiring Decisions

When we interview potential employees, every member of our team has the chance to meet and evaluate them in a one-on-one interview. It's only fair since they will be working and collaborating closely with them. We also do group interviews. This can be intimidating for the job seeker, but you get a chance to see how they relate and their personal style. We do all of this before I talk with the individual. It's a strategy that has interesting benefits.

First, you can get a good read on a person if they are put off by not getting to talk to the boss or decision-maker out of the gate. You get insights from your team because they are looking for different things than you are as the head of the organization. And there is huge value in including your existing team in decisions that drive the business. They feel and act more like owners when you let them participate in the interview process.

But we don't stop there. We generally ask a candidate to work with us for a day or so, and we pay them. This is an effective way to see if they can be a part of the team and use their skills. Anyone can keep up a good front during an interview; it's harder to do that for a day or so. You also see how well they perform under stress.

This system works, and I often suggest it to other business owners. One of the few times I did not take my own advice and dispensed with using this process, it was a disaster. I was in one of those knee-jerk reaction modes, and we needed to fill a spot for an employee who moved away. One recent graduate looked so promising that I simply hired him. After sixty days, he sauntered into my office and announced he was moving back home—the job was just too hard. I told him that's why they call it work. The experience cost us dearly. We wasted time interviewing him, we wasted money moving him, and we wasted effort on training. The cost of hiring the wrong person is significant, so it's important to get it right—for both the employer and the potential employee.

Make Room for Those with Great Potential

Sometimes you run across a potential good fit for your organization when you aren't even looking. It's tempting to dismiss a job seeker when you don't have an opening, but you might want to think a bit differently. It might be forward-thinking to create a position when you find a talented person. I have done that on a number of occasions. One individual who cold-called our office was so impressive over the phone that I interviewed and hired him, even though we did not have an opening. He has been with me for over twenty-two years. Employees who get in early and grow with a company can have very profitable careers and even end up as shareholders.

The big question is how to afford an individual when you don't have a budgeted position. Here you need to get creative. I have taken temporary pay cuts to bring someone on board. I know other business owners who have used a credit line to fund a position initially. If it is a sales position, you can offer a small base, plus commission, so that the individual is paying for themselves. Remember, you are taking a long-term view of the business when you bring in those with great potential, so you might need to make some short-term adjustments.

Be a Solopreneur

While I have spent a great deal of time talking about hiring the right people, there is one additional option to consider. I believe that employees are critical to my business. That is not always the case. Solopreneur is one of the newer ideas in entrepreneurship. The trend is named by putting two words together—solo and entrepreneur. It is different from being a freelancer. A solopreneur is someone who designs and builds a business that they can operate alone. A solopreneur generally has a number of different revenue streams. They don't just sell their time; they have products or activities that make them money even when they are not working. I think it takes a very motivated and organized individual to be a solopreneur. They don't have employees to back them up.

For those who don't want to manage people and deal with turnover and the other issues related to HR, this can be a great option. You can still hire contractors to do certain things but only when you need them. An added benefit is that in today's digital world, you have access to lots of amazing talent right at your fingertips. Of course, solopreneurs can grow into entrepreneurs over time.

The Right External Team

The concept of hiring the right people at the right time extends to your external team as well. There are a couple of different types of external teams. One is the traditional team you hire; the other is one you access for their expertise, and they look and act like in-house employees, but they are not. You are outsourcing that job.

Marilyn Landis believes that small-business owners may want to outsource everything except their core competency. She points to encore entrepreneurs. These are generally individuals from the boomer generation who are turning to small-business ownership. Says Landis:

> These individuals have great expertise. They don't want to go to work for somebody on their payroll. So you suddenly have this whole raft of very seasoned professionals available who want to be your outsource location for HR, or IT, or ISO 9000, or whatever it happens to be. I have a client in Cleveland, and her entire C-suite, or corporate executive suite, is outsourced. I'm her CFO. She's got her marketing person, she's got her IT, she's got her ISO 9000, and she's got her HR professional. This allows her to bring the highest expertise to the table when she needs it.[1]

Of course, there are still the traditional advisors that you use regularly or on an as-needed basis. These are the individuals that every business needs to advise and guide throughout the life of the organization. This is not a place to skimp, because you get what you pay for. But to be clear, your needs may change so that team might need to change. In fact, that is almost a given, but I see business owners staying with an attorney or accountant because of misplaced loyalty. Some of your paid professionals may stay with you after the start-up. Others can provide specific short-term expertise to jump-start your efforts but are not needed long term. Who are these individuals, and how do you find them?

I sought out some of my start-up team. Others found their way to me through business contacts. Some of the team may be obvious, others are not. The attorney who helped me set up the company did such a great job that we were able to use a younger and less expensive attorney during the buyout of my partner. By choosing a firm with great depth, we are never "over-lawyered" or "under-lawyered." We get the level of service we need when we need it. A good law firm will help set the foundation of your business for start-up and beyond. And if they do not have the expertise you need, they should get you to the right person to help.

When it comes to an accountant, the right person is not just someone who understands numbers but someone who really understands business. There is a difference. Many accountants do the typical work of monthly and quarterly statements, tax returns, and the like. But you need someone who goes way beyond that. You need someone who understands the vision of your business and can help guide you. I sought out someone who specialized in small business. In fact, he was incredibly involved with the statewide and national associations and advocated for small business. Your accountant should be more than a number cruncher. An accountant should be a trusted resource.

While that accountant served my business well, things changed. The accountant retired and sold the business to an associate. At first things went well, but it did not last. I started to find that filings were being delayed, questions were not getting answered in a timely manner. I was loyal, and that is not always the best thing. After a few years, it became obvious that the level of expertise and service was not there right at a time when we were growing.

I set out on a search to interview other accounting firms. I eventually hired a new one, and only then did I realize that we had areas that were not being addressed and that some of the work was just "sloppy." Fortunately, the new firm did an excellent job and got us back on track. The lesson here is to be sure that every few years you get a "second opinion" and have an outside source look at the work. Don't stay with a firm out of blind loyalty. Do your homework, because the survival of your business depends on it.

The right "banker" should also be a person or organization that does more than take care of your financial needs. They should be concerned about helping you make business connections. I'm not just talking about networking. I am talking about helping you connect with businesses that you want to target. They should also help you connect with other business owners in meaningful ways, such as in forums, community discussions, and so on. I believe you should look for a financial institution that is very involved in the community. Not just sponsoring events, although that is great, but also lending their expertise, and their people, to civic and non-profit organizations.

An area where most of us need help is human resources. I was fortunate enough to get guidance from an HR professional who was a friend of the family. He got me started on the essentials—developing basic policies and procedures, an employee handbook, and basic benefits. Today, it is much more complicated, and the world is more litigious. In the past, business owners thought they needed to have an HR professional on staff; now, there are many more options. You can get help if you are a member of a local or statewide organization. They often prequalify resources, and you may get some free or discounted services. When looking for HR help, you should know that there are two types of HR professionals. One is an HR adminis-trator. This individual can help you with things like benefits, compensation, and compliance. There are also organizational design consultants. They concentrate on performance management, culture, and coaching. By using these professionals on an as-needed basis, you will be prepared to deal with anything that might arise in this area.

Hiring the right insurance specialist or real estate professional is also critical. Big business knows how to access resources to assess their risk exposures, and they usually have expert insurance and risk-management professionals. The reason is obvious: big business is acutely aware of the devastating effect catastrophic losses have on the bottom line. When you are a small company, it is just as important. In fact, your big customers will insist that you have taken steps to manage risk because *your* "risky behavior" can increase *their* risk exposure. Often, small-business owners rely on anecdotal advice from peers in their industries regarding their insurance needs, instead of engaging an insurance or risk-management professional and educating themselves on their own individual insurance-program needs.

In the early years, some small businesses treat insurance as optional, rather than as a critical expense. They feel they can purchase it down the road, when cash flow improves, and their exposure is larger. This is just plain dumb. It makes you and your customers more vulnerable to loss in many ways. More and more often, my customers are asking to see certificates of insurance and understand the depth and capability of my supply chain. I am also conscious that any disruption to my business, even for a day or two, can be disastrous. It means I can't deliver what I have promised, and that affects my customer's ability to deliver. You don't need to know it all. You do need to find an insurance agent or risk-management professional you can trust.

Whether the right people are internal or external, you need to hire them at the right time. If you don't, you miss opportunities to connect with and win big business. If you run so lean that customers feel like you are always frantic, you will not inspire confidence. And customers won't send more business your way or recommend you to others. If you have the right people in place, you become known as the expert, and you can take on more business with ease.

TIPS TO SUCCEED

▸ Don't wait until you are overwhelmed to hire. Use nontraditional methods to find the right person.

▸ The right person for a small business looks very different from the right person for a big business.

- ▸ Involve your employees in the hiring process.

- ▸ Pay attention to onboarding; it's more than an orientation.

- ▸ Think about outsourcing. Will it work for you? What can you outsource?

SUCCEED AT OPERATIONS

7

YOU ARE THE BOSS.
NOW WHAT?

You thought about it, dreamed about it, and now you are the boss. If you worked for someone for any period of time, you probably said, "When I am the boss, things will be different." Only when you take on the role do you fully realize that running a successful business is tough. I know, because I established and have successfully led my company for over thirty-five years. There were days when I was tired, discouraged, and overwhelmed. But I never wanted to quit, and I can tell you that the sacrifice and struggle have been worth the effort. Staying in has taught me a lot of lessons. It has also helped me be more confident and courageous.

Starting and running a business exposes you to financial risk, criticism, and sometimes legal obstacles. So you need to figure out how to be more than just a traditional boss. You need to be a leader, and leading a small business is much different from a larger company. That's because you often don't have others on your staff at your level. In a book I coauthored entitled *Stop Wishing. Stop Whining. Start Leading.*, we detailed eleven traits that are critical to the success of leaders.

Five Important Leadership Qualities

I talked at great length earlier in this book about having passion for your business. That is certainly needed in the early phases, when you face the fear of failure and often discouraging times as you hit bumps in the road. Laser focus is another trait that you must have as the boss. While others can get distracted, you can't afford to get sidetracked. You have to keep your eye on the operation and help employees solve problems. Problems, or challenges, are often more prevalent in start-ups when systems and processes are not fully formed. You need to stay calm and bring others to the table to focus on and simplify complex issues. Here are the qualities that I believe can make you a more desirable boss at start-up and for the long haul.

Vision

To begin, you need to be the chief strategy officer, the visionary that sets the tone for the business. Visionary leaders are vastly different. In the past, leaders were like generals who wanted to command and control people. That rarely works, especially with younger workers who want to be inspired.

So where does the vision come from? Lots of places. Visionary leaders are constantly searching for and tracking sources of information and inspiration. They watch what is happening in the world. They read journals and join other leaders to advocate for small business. If you are a visionary, you know that it is about more than just your business, it is about impacting your entire industry.

Want to be a good boss? Design a picture of where the company is going and invite people to come along.

Courage

As the boss, you are responsible for everything. Have you ever been frustrated while waiting for a decision? In larger companies, it can sometimes take what seems like forever to see movement. As the boss of a smaller organization, you need to be courageous when it comes to making decisions. And do that every day. You should never float ideas to get a reaction. I will say more about this in chapter 9. For now, know that I consider floating ideas as one of the top seven communication mistakes.

Unfortunately, it is a common practice in some organizations and is even encouraged. Yes, there is a time for that, but as the boss you need to do more. Do your research and get input from your trusted advisors or others who have experience. You never have all the information you need, but you can't wait forever, or you get left behind. Make a timely decision that is right for the organization. The truth is, you might be wrong—you would not be the first.

Not making a decision *is* a decision. It also goes without saying that you should not be afraid to make tough decisions, even if it makes you unpopular. That is the sign of a good leader. People will get on board once they see how your decision plays out.

Responsibility

At a small company, you know every employee—it's personal. I know that I, and most owners, feel a huge responsibility for employees. I know their families. I know their challenges. To maintain a healthy business, you need to really care about employees but at the same time be able to balance that with doing what is best for the whole organization. You take on the responsibility for the culture, quality of the work, the profits—everything.

It's bound to happen. One of your employees will do something or say something that causes trouble. A good boss takes the hit for the organization. They don't blame others. They step up and take responsibility, even if they did not make the decision or the mistake. When employees know you have their back, they are willing to do anything for you—that is a gift.

Resiliency

Doing business today can be chaotic. Pandemics. Interruptions to the supply chain. The labor shortage. Robert Kennedy once said, "If there's nobody in your way, it's because you're not going anywhere." When you hit a roadblock, fall flat on your face, or encounter any number of other setbacks, how do you react?

When you're the boss, being resilient is part of the job. Can you bounce back? What do you do when a customer fires you? How do you react under pressure or criticism? Are you quick-thinking, especially in emergencies or crisis situations? When a crisis happens, you must think and solve the problem quickly because people are depending on you. It is crucial to maintain a clear head and focus, set emotion and fear aside, sort the information available, and rapidly reach a solution.

Humility

I learned early on the importance of humility, and I keep learning that lesson. As the boss, you need to focus on getting the job done, on your mission and vision, on doing the best for your company, employees, and customers. It is not about you! It is not about being recognized or enhancing your image. People are attracted to those who are authentically humble. And it is a character quality that you can cultivate.

Books such as *Leaders Eat Last* by Simon Sinek and *Leadership Is an Art* by Max DePree explore the topic of leadership in great depth. I like to think of it this way. When it comes to leading, choose to go last instead of pushing to be first. Be willing to take criticism and admit when you are wrong. Ask for help instead of pretending to know it all. There is great power in saying, "I don't know."

When others praise you, share the praise with your team. I believe that employees will go above and beyond when you show that you are doing your very best, not grabbing the spotlight or boasting about your accomplishments. When you are arrogant and rude, you are not a boss that anyone wants to work for.

Being the Boss Is an Art

Do you wonder how some people just seem to know how to be the boss while others feel uncomfortable in the role? Are you born to be the boss? Can you learn to be a good boss? There are many stories about terrible ones. I heard someone recently say that people don't leave companies, they leave their boss. That may be an oversimplification, but there is truth in that statement.

The Emmy award–winning *Undercover Boss* is a TV reality show. In this series, the boss gets out of the office and goes undercover to take a lower-level job. The boss learns things about their organization that they did not know, and for most it is life changing. The show is quite touching but also formulaic. The boss, who has obviously lost touch with their organization, gets a wake-up call. That's good, but how did that boss get so far away from the reality of the workplace? How did it get to the point at which they had to go undercover to see what was really happening? This is great television. The boss becomes enlightened. The workers feel appreciated. Things change for the better. There is a happy ending. I find it a little sad. If we want to be good leaders, we should try to ensure that we stay close to the organization, even as the business grows. Yes, it is harder, but it is worth the effort.

What I have observed is that, like so many other things in life, being the boss is a balance between art and science. There are basic good practices, such as setting goals and objectives for your team, learning problem-solving techniques, listening to employees and advisors, and appropriately delegating tasks. These are some of the themes from *Undercover Boss*. But the *art* of being a boss is harder to explain.

For me it is personal. To be a good boss, you have to care. Care about your people. Care about their families. Care about their struggles and help them succeed. Care about the quality of the product or service. Care about the customers. I know what you are thinking. "With all that caring, it has to be exhausting." Not if you are a good boss.

Don't Go It Alone

You have heard the saying, "It's lonely at the top." It does not have to be. There are so many resources available to those who need to develop new skills or leadership insights. The first step is to know when you are in over your head and need some help. Are you stressed, overworked, frustrated, scared, confused, or angry? Are you facing immediate challenges and need to develop strategies to move forward? Do you need a support system?

The best resource for a business owner is another business owner. I have developed a network of small-business owners just by attending local events. These are my "go to" resources when I need quick advice. Some states have organizations specifically for small business. Some have a broad membership of diverse businesses. Others are focused on a specific industry or profession. Look for the ones that have advocacy and education as part of their mission. Some organizations focus on networking. That is fine, but you are more likely to find help when there are educational events and sharing forums.

One example of an organization that leads in this area is Primerus, an international association of small and medium-sized law firms. They say that Primerus members are "good people who happen to be good lawyers." These are firms that specialize in various specific legal areas, often called boutique firms. They are not "the big guys" and don't have the resources of larger firms. But they are arguably some of the world's finest law firms.

I have worked with this organization, and it is impressive the level of support they provide to members. In addition to conferences and events, they offer a webinar series called *Coffee and Conversation*. Individual members host webinars and share their knowledge about timely topics such as mentoring, business succession, using technology, and more. In the process, they all learn to become better personally and professionally. Members also have many peer groups, including ones for young lawyers and women lawyers.

For more formal assistance, facilitated peer-to-peer groups are an amazing source of knowledge and support. These can be accessed through local chambers or statewide business organizations. The US Small Business Administration also has a network of partners across the country that offer free or low-cost counseling or training. Just go to *sba.gov* and put in your zip code to find a resource. Or use their online resources to write a business plan, calculate start-up costs, or get free small-business data and trends.

A Final Thought

One final thought. There is a difference between being the boss and being a leader. If you are a boss, people *must* follow you. If you are a leader, people *choose* to follow you. You don't just suddenly become a great leader. It is actually a lifelong journey, and nothing can take the place of practicing the traits I have outlined in the chapter. This is just the start. Go beyond being just the boss. Be a leader, and your small business will thrive.

TIPS TO SUCCEED

- ▸ Take some time to consider your personal strengths and areas that need work.

- ▸ Write down some of the typical activities that you perform and how you will do them as a leader rather than as a boss.

- ▸ Build or grow a network of leaders who can help you grow personally and professionally.

8
WHERE AND HOW TO WORK SMARTER

Business owners spend a great deal of time thinking about and developing their products and services. They often don't stop to consider whether their actual workplace is working for them. Or where people are working. It may be the kitchen table, a local coffee shop, a car, or the office. The choices are many. The reality is that the workplace is changing. Some are still in the office or store from nine to five. Others who work from home, or went home during the pandemic, might never return. And then there are hybrid workers. Today's businesses are struggling to find the balance, and, depending upon the type of work, the answers can vary dramatically.

Transitioning from Home to Office

I started my business working out of my home. It was a good move financially because, among other things, it freed up cash to buy equipment. For a while it worked. I had a home office and used space on the lower level for equipment storage. I generally went to the client's location to work, so I didn't need to worry about a meeting space. It wasn't too long before I outgrew my home office. As I added equipment and started to think about hiring employees, it became obvious—I had to look for a facility. Since then, we have moved several times as our needs and the business have changed.

Today, my staff works mostly from the office when not traveling, and some individuals work from home as needed. One of the things we have done to provide flexibility is to ensure that people have the technology to allow them to be productive no matter where they are working. We have provided bigger monitors for their home offices. We have also purchased subscriptions for software that makes them more productive. While many of our face-to-face encounters are now virtual, we still need to provide opportunities for people to gather. Gathering has huge benefits. It makes collaboration easy. No need to schedule a meeting to review a project. No need to put off that simple question—you get answers immediately. There's an energy that comes from the workplace when everyone is busy, and the office is humming.

Over the years, we have worked in a few different locations. The changes have been driven by the work we are doing. For example, we worked out of our own building for almost fifteen years. It was great, but as time went on, we were spending more time out of the office—on planes to visit our clients or to shoot videos on location. There were times when only one person was left all alone in the office. So why did we need all that space?

In the early days, we did much of our work in our studio in the building. In later years, that studio was used infrequently. Recently, we downsized and sold the building. We now work out of a smaller leased space that is closer to the airport. That's where we are headed every week, and the convenience has been amazing. While the space is smaller, it still works, and I would argue that going from individual offices to an open plan has done a lot for communication. So how do you decide to make changes in how and where you work? It's complicated. But here are a few questions that I believe every business owner should ask from time to time.

- Has your business experienced changes that require adjustments to the workplace? Do you really need all that space?

- Does the current physical structure work? If not, can it be changed to meet the needs of the workflow?

- Does the environment meet your technological needs? Do you have reliable high-speed internet? Checked upload and download speeds?

- Does the current configuration speed up communication, collaboration, and decision-making?

- How many of your staff can or want to work from home?

- What are the costs associated with change, such as new furniture, installation of new equipment, and downtime?

- Do you regularly host clients at your location? Does the space project an image that is positive for the business? Will your customers be impressed by your workplace?

- Do you even need an office?

These are puzzling questions, and the answers change quickly.

Does Your Space Reflect the Way You Work?

One of the big trends in offices is the move to more comfortable and collaborative spaces. The famous cubicles from the past are quickly disappearing. Instead, casual furniture groupings as a place to meet are designed to spur creativity. Big meetings are replaced by stand-up "huddles" and quick catch-ups, so big conference rooms are also on the way out. And as more people are spread across the country, virtual meetings are the norm. That's why you are seeing more spaces that are designed to be small but are technology rich.

There are things that have not changed. The small-business owner wants their space to be welcoming, a good reflection of their brand. This is especially important for retail operations and some service businesses. I believe no matter what the environment, you need to make a smart investment, a quality product that is affordable and looks great. There are places where you should not skimp. For example, if it is an office setting, you need really good chairs and ergonomically supportive workspaces. Yes, I know that sounds like a little thing, but with the amount of time people spend working on computers, it is important.

Safety and security are increasingly important in the workplace. Today, even smaller companies are taking measures to ensure that there are systems in place to keep workers safe. That means installing lighting in parking areas and halls. Motion sensors are a simple way to light up areas. Building systems now allow for keycard or code access so that doors do not need to be left unlocked, inviting unwanted guests. Security monitoring systems are not expensive and are worth the peace of mind.

In addition, building systems can help regulate cooling and heating, as well as program preferred comfort settings. This is especially important when people spend hours in meetings. Why? People are more productive when they are comfortable. Not to mention, when you only light, cool, or heat a room when occupied, you save energy.

Office Trends

Another trend that deserves careful consideration is balancing time in the office with work-at-home or hybrid employees. There are lots of ideas about the value of these arrangements, as well as lots of skepticism. This is a complex issue that all companies face, and there is research to guide you. I would not presume to tell anyone how to manage this situation. How do you decide who can work from home? How many days? Should everyone get the same number of days at home? These are just a few of the issues. I will offer observations from my own experience, as well as the experience of my customers.

First, not everyone can be productive while working a hybrid schedule. Many workers need the structure of the office to be productive. Conditions such as others in the home who are also working a hybrid schedule, children or elderly parents living at home, the lack of privacy, or many other distractions can take a toll. For newer workers, it can be difficult to make business connections that help them get up to speed. They miss out on the culture of the office and can feel isolated. Finally, some people simply do not have the self-discipline to work at home.

Second, do you have the systems in place to assure good communication when people are working from home? Do you have a consistent way to stay in touch? Do you have the tools (Slack, Teams, etc.) to be sure that it is easy to communicate and collaborate?

Third, how do you make the most of the time when people *are* in the office? Do you have good productive meetings or activities, so it is worth the time to travel to the office?

If you are a very small business with just a few employees, you may not need to be concerned about creating a great space or hybrid work. I have counseled some business owners to never get an office, to continue to work at home but improve that space. Today there are endless choices for home offices and resources to help you design one. You don't need to spend a great deal of money. You do need to be sure that the workspace . . . works!

For those who do not need a space all the time, there are more options now than in the past. Building developers and builders have options for shared space. Some may offer you your own dedicated area, access to common spaces and technology for virtual meetings, and other amenities. Others have spaces that you can use on a first-come, first-served basis. You may not always be in the same place, but maybe that's good and can jump-start new and creative thinking. One thing is certain: Situations are always changing, so your workplace needs to change as well. I believe that creating a great workspace will always be a good investment.

TIPS TO SUCCEED

- ▸ Assess the need for space and decide how employees can be most productive and happy. In office? At home? Hybrid?

- ▸ Businesses with great environments generally have higher profits, better employee engagement, and a stronger brand.

- ▸ Employee health and wellness are directly related to the work environment.

9
CONNECT.
COMMUNICATE.
CONVINCE.

B efore I became a business owner, I worked in broadcasting. During my thirteen years in the business, I had the chance to connect and communicate with a broad range of individuals, from CEOs of major corporations to those on the factory floor. It was a wonderful job because I got to see the good, the bad, and the ugly ways that people communicate—or don't.

Many organizations don't recognize the need for communication; it is not a priority. Or it is way down the list of priorities. They assume it will happen naturally, organically. Unfortunately, that is not the case. Have you ever heard someone say, "Nobody told me"? I have, and it happens more often than leaders wish to admit. I have watched companies experience the impact of communications that got sidetracked, causing a loss of productivity, profitability, and employee engagement. The consequences are real; 86 percent of employees and executives cite the lack of effective collaboration and communication as the main causes for workplace failures.[1]

Communication is critical—personally and professionally. But as the famous playwright George Bernard Shaw stated, "The biggest problem with communication is the illusion that it has taken place." Unfortunately, the saying still holds true today. The problem is not unusual, and it impacts everyone along your business supply chain, from your vendors to employees to customers and stakeholders.

Lots of business owners and managers complain that they are working with terrible communicators. Often those same leaders do not understand their role in communication. To make things even worse, they may not hire people who have the necessary skills to design and deliver important communication programs. As a result, employees don't understand what they are supposed to do. They are left to their own devices and then get reprimanded because they did not do the "right thing." When communication is poor, people get left out of the planning process. They don't get invited to or bother to attend meetings where they are needed. They don't offer up ideas because they do not think anyone will listen. Some of the best ideas come from those on the front lines, people who have the most knowledge and exposure to the work. Without their input, it is easy to make decisions in a vacuum. Ask yourself, are we really communicating, or are we under the illusion that good communication has taken place?

The Changing Landscape

Look around the workplace today and you see forces at work that have changed the communication landscape. For the first time in history, there are five generations working side by side, from the Silent Generation to Gen Z. They care about different things. They have different work styles. They communicate differently. That is an understatement.

At the same time, the speed of work is often at a breakneck pace. Everyone wants everything now. Without precise, complete communication, it is easy to make mistakes. There are a variety of communication channels—email, instant messaging, live chat, text, phone, and face to face. That can cause communication confusion. It is especially difficult when one individual has a preferred method of communication, say email, and another wants a face-to-face interaction.

How do you accommodate the wide range of individuals and leverage communication to make your operation successful? It starts with those at the top of the organization. I believe that leaders have a special and unique responsibility when it comes to communication. We are held to a higher standard and what we say matters—inside our company and outside.

The first thing you must do is make communication a priority. That means being available to connect. I see leaders who make every budget meeting, but when it comes time to visit an employee meeting, they run late or stop in but don't really engage. Employees are hungry to be "in the know." They want to hear from leaders and have the chance to ask questions. The same is true of customers. How do you connect and communicate with individuals of every generation? It is not easy. You need to pay attention to the basics and avoid common communication mistakes.

Seven Common Communication Mistakes

Here are the seven most common communication mistakes leaders can make.

Inconsistent Communication

People get nervous when they don't hear from you, or your representatives, on a consistent basis. That might mean weekly, biweekly, or maybe even every day if there is a need. Some only communicate when things go wrong. That is a huge mistake. Communicate good and bad news on a regular basis. Have a schedule and stick to it.

Muddy Messages

What are muddy messages? They are the ones with no clear purpose. Information that has not been analyzed and synthesized. This is when people just do a brain dump and hope that the listener gets something.

Messages must be purposeful. Otherwise, why are you communicating? Think about what you are trying to get the listener to do. Everything must support that. Muddy messages also have no examples to help people understand the content in the context of the workplace.

For example, if you just say, "We need to improve," people have no idea what to do to make the needed improvements. If you say, "Ten percent of our orders are incomplete when they ship. We are going to train everyone on our new tracking system and aim for 100 percent accuracy within thirty days." Now the message is crystal clear. Don't confuse people and leave them wondering what action to take.

Ignoring Your Audience

Don't tell people what *you want* to tell them. Tell them what *they need* to know to be able to contribute to the organization, improve their performance, and move themselves to a higher level. It is important to share your vision, tell a relevant story or personal experience, and offer powerful illustrations.

But remember that the individual listening is thinking, "What's in it for me?" Make sure that your content flows logically and use lots of great examples that apply to them to clarify the point. Pick out "wow" statistics to bolster your message. When you are passionate about the business, it inspires those listening. When it comes to great communication, it is not about you.

Probably the best example I can share is the CEO who visited a company location shortly after firing the general manager. He completely ignored the fact that the facility was "leaderless" and talked about new initiatives. Employees were stunned, and no one felt comfortable asking questions. The audience needed answers, to hear the plan for the facility. Instead, they were ignored.

Thinking One Size Fits All

In the early stages of a business, your organization may be simple, but as you grow, it becomes more complicated and diverse. Your communication needs to evolve. Are you sending out communications and "blasting" everyone in the organization? Think about whether the information is of value to all. Sure, there are things that everyone needs to know, but too often we invite people to meetings they don't need to attend. Or copy them on emails when they do not need to be involved. Communication must be targeted to be effective. That means giving the right information to the right people, at the right time. If you overwhelm people with information they don't need and cannot use, they tune you out.

You also need to consider the language you use with different "audiences." Those in different departments or individuals at various levels of the organization need language that applies directly to them. Think about the complexity of what you are saying, the tone, and adjust accordingly.

The "one-size-fits-all" mistake also applies to customers and partners. External communication must be targeted as well. Some factors to consider are the length of association. The way you communicate with long-term partners is quite different from those with a newer relationship. With newer individuals, you must be more detailed and clearer. Always check to discover their preferred channels of communication. Finally, remember the goal—to connect and convince.

Floating Balloons

Consider a floating balloon. It goes one way then another, carried by the wind. It has no clear direction.

Some organizations use informal communication to try out ideas and see if they rise to the top. I am not talking about brainstorming a solution or having an open discussion about issues. I am talking about the practice of leaking information to see if the reaction is positive or negative. An example of this might be leaking information about a plan to combine two departments. Or testing the waters to see if there is pushback on adjusting work hours or calling remote workers back. Those who use this technique appear weak and aimless. No one wants to feel that the individual or organization they work for does not have a solid plan and simply blows in the wind without purpose.

Using Corporate Speak

Leaders who use lots of jargon, overused phrases, and meaningless words in an effort to appear important are not effective communicators. If you just simply spout the same thing that everyone else is saying, in the same way, there is nothing to set you apart.

I think people use "corporate speak" because they believe it makes them sound smarter or more important. They say things such as, "We're focused on the future. We are collaborating with our partners to win together. We must be transparent in all aspects of our operation so we can be operationally excellent and leverage best practices."

The problem is that these phrases could apply to any company, anywhere. They are too general. They lack vision, passion, energy, conviction, and imagination. If employees and customers feel that you offer nothing new and do not present anything that challenges them, you will lose their attention and engagement.

Lack of Enthusiasm

If you are not enthusiastic, others see that. If you speak in a monotone voice, lack facial expression, or don't have energy, you are seen as disinterested. And if you are not interested, why should employees or customers care? If you are late to meetings, are not prepared, or don't follow through with initiatives, you will be viewed as ineffective or irrelevant.

Sometimes, senior leaders commit these leadership errors in the mistaken view that their seniority gives them the "right" to relax standards for themselves. Nothing could be further from the truth, and no one wants to work for or with a leader who lacks enthusiasm and engagement. If you want more attention, be more interesting! Stop boring others with poor communication.

One last word about communication mistakes. In business, you must have multiple channels, opportunities, and methods of communication. This is the key. It must also be a two-way system. If you do not have a built-in mechanism for "listening," you will never be a communicator that can convince others to contribute.

Meetings and More

I am not a huge fan of meetings, but I do love the concept of "huddles." I often use the huddle to kick off the day. With a staff of ten or fewer, it's easy to do a quick catch-up. We look at the week. What do we need to accomplish, can we celebrate some sensational work or effort, what do we need to improve or fix? A huddle needs to be timely, upbeat, and give everyone a chance to report out. If you have larger organizations, you might have monthly or quarterly meetings. Here is a tip. Schedule them far enough out and stick to the schedule. For those who are unable to attend, send a written follow-up.

Leaders must be out front at meetings and communicate with power. What does that mean? Think about inspirational leaders you have seen in the media. How do they capture your attention? They certainly are not boring.

Zippia is a technology company that works to help people improve their career outcomes. They have done a great deal of research into the workplace.

I am not surprised by what they found. They surveyed employees about meetings and discovered that "45% of employees feel overwhelmed by the number of meetings they attend [and] 39% of employees surveyed have slept during a work meeting. And that figure is even worse for daydreaming, as at least 91% of employees daydream during work meetings."[2]

Those numbers are amazingly consistent with previous studies by other organizations over the years. Why haven't they improved? It is simple. We don't take the time to communicate. And when we do, we fall prey to the common mistakes I have outlined here.

TIPS TO SUCCEED

- ▶ The business landscape is changing, and you need to accommodate different generations.

- ▶ There are common communication mistakes that can be avoided.

- ▶ Internal and external communication has different content and audiences.

- ▶ Stop boring people with poor communication. Instead connect, communicate, and convince.

10

WHEN IT COMES TO OPERATIONS, THINK LIKE A BIG BUSINESS

When it comes to operations, it's easy for small-business owners to consider themselves minor players. Because they're small, they think they don't need the systems, procedures, and safeguards that huge companies have in place. Actually, it is very important for small businesses to have these systems, because there are fewer people to shoulder the work.

Have a System for Everything

So where are some of the areas to think big? According to Bob Fish, it is every aspect of the business. He says, "I really do believe in systematizing everything. Take what is routine and mundane and create a system around it. Then anybody can execute it. That frees up your mind to take care of the vision, and whatever is important to the company."[1] There are some things that are easy to systematize in the coffee business, such as how to make an espresso, but Fish says others are not so obvious:

> We have a system for how to greet a customer; how to have a chat with a customer at the end of the counter, and so on. The systems end

up becoming the playbook for the company. A company needs that playbook or roadmap. Without it, we're just a bunch of individuals, and we might all go in different directions. But because we're tied together by a system, it's what allows us to grow so fast.[2]

At Cynthia Kay and Company, we also believe in having systems in place. In fact, we have documented, step by step, almost all of our processes and procedures. For example, there are endless types and sizes of video files. We have created profiles for each of our clients so that we know exactly what to provide them each time, no matter who is working on the project. When a specification for a customer changes, we document it. It's important to have one central location where you put all your documentation. Everything needs to be easy for everyone to find and update.

We also use time-tracking programs so we can accurately report to our clients where we are with regard to the budget. We use an electronic dashboard to track every project, including where it is in the process ("on fire" means we are on deadline), who is working on it, any special instructions, and more. We also have a system for how all field equipment should be packed and stored. That way everyone knows where it is every time, and we won't accidentally leave anything behind when we go out to a jobsite.

Think about Quality and Delivery

Of course, just because you have a system in place does not mean that you are producing a quality product or service or that you can deliver on time. If you want to attract and retain big customers, you have to assure them that your quality will not be an issue or put their brand at risk. According to Mark Peters, CEO of Butterball Farms, Inc.:

> The biggest driver for big, especially branded, companies is brand risk. We now have an international certification for our quality systems. You simply have to do the hard work to be sure that you will not put your customer's brand at risk, whether that is by not delivering, or a safety issue, or a quality standard issue. A lot of small companies don't get that. They come in with a product, but they don't understand how the other pieces of their business put their customer's brand at risk. And so they don't get asked to the table.[3]

Charles Phaneuf, the former owner of CE Rental, agrees with Peters, and offers three tricks that helped his operation. He says:

Quality has to be the primary operational outcome, and cost has to be close behind to continue operating. Quality brings customers back. Cost control keeps pricing competitive and keeps us alive to be there for the returning customer. When an operation gets to a point that it produces a quality outcome at a competitive cost, the first trick is to "lock it in" to get the desired result to repeat. Then, like a big company, the entrepreneur can define a process, function, or job, and hand it off to an employee so the entrepreneur can move on to the next process or function that needs to be defined, debugged, and developed. Slowly, the entrepreneur builds structure that can carry on and function independent of the entrepreneur, much like a big company. The second trick is to remain close to the operation and continue to measure results and evolve those processes or functions. The third trick is to get the organization to monitor and improve itself by training employees to think and act like entrepreneurs. Then the entrepreneur has something that won't be a burden to operate and is saleable, if and when the entrepreneur is ready.[4]

Go Digital

Digitalization is touching every aspect of our world and changing our personal and professional lives. In the business world, "going digital" means looking for ways to be more efficient, lower your costs, and just make it easier to do business with larger entities. For a small company going digital, there are many opportunities around operations. You can use technology to transform your processes, redesign products and services, or even change the way you distribute what you make. There are so many ways to transform your business that entire volumes have been written.

For those in the manufacturing area, Industry 4.0 provides a path to digital transformation. For others, going digital may mean looking at ecommerce, moving from paper-based systems to the cloud, or finding new ways to improve customer service. My one caution is this: Small businesses need to have a plan and gear up slowly. You need to understand why transformation is necessary and how you will measure success. Otherwise, you will spend money without knowing if the changes are right for the organization. We will focus on technology in chapter 17.

Think Lean

Many big companies spend time and money for studies showing how to eliminate waste and become more efficient. It's called "lean," and it has its roots in a system designed by Toyota. Since then, manufacturers, healthcare organizations, and others have adopted the principles. But this strategy is not just for big organizations. I was first introduced to the concept by a number of my clients. I paid attention and started to think about how it could be applied on a smaller scale to Cynthia Kay and Company.

My company consistently evaluates our processes, and we make changes to be more efficient. It does not take much to figure out what you need to change. Just look at the areas of your business where you are experiencing a bottleneck or wasted time. You don't need to do a big study. You do, though, need to ask questions of your employees and search for solutions. However, it's not always about *doing* something; sometimes it's best *not* to do anything.

For example, we used to track every activity in our media production process. That was time-consuming, so we decided to prioritize the activities and only track those that had a real impact on the work. By eliminating some of the busywork of tracking nonessential tasks, we have more time to concentrate on the important aspects of our business. One thing to note: ask your customers what is important to them. Take that information and be sure to track or provide what they need. It might seem insignificant to you, but they may have very definite requirements, and you need to be aware of them.

Big businesses routinely use outside resources. This is an area where my organization thinks big, too. Do we really need to be employment specialists? Do we need to be accounting and tax specialists? Do we need to be IT professionals? The answer is no. That's why we have put into place the resources that help our operation become leaner, better, and more efficient.

How well you operate your business is important to your customers. You need to be sure that things run smoothly so you don't let them down.

TIPS TO SUCCEED

- ▶ Have a system for everything; it becomes the playbook for your organization.

- ▶ Document all your critical processes and procedures and keep the information in one central location.

- ▶ Look for opportunities to go digital.

- ▶ Think lean. Eliminate waste in your systems and become efficient so you can respond quickly.

11
FIND YOUR COMPANY VOICE

Every company has a personality, a style. You might not think much about it, but you should, because it can make the difference between standing out from the crowd or getting lost in the noise. Having a company voice:

- ensures message consistency
- aligns everyone with company goals
- engages employees
- drives business

So, what exactly is a company voice . . . and how do you find it? Before we jump into that, you need to briefly understand branding or a brand. It is a complex topic, so let me make it simple by using some examples. Some powerful examples of brands are Apple, Starbucks, Coca-Cola, Gerber, and Uber. We all know what they do and what they make. But brand is about more than that. It's about the people of the company, who they are, what they care about, and the mission that drives them.

Brand is a perception. You can't see it or touch it. There are intangible elements that give people a feeling or a connection to your product, service, or organization. Elements that contribute to the perception include the tone of your messages and marks such as logos, icons, and fonts.

Your company voice is about how you communicate your brand to your "audience," which includes everyone from employees and stakeholders to suppliers and customers—really, anyone who is in your circle of influence.

Some think that public relations or advertising is what tells your story. That is part of it, but there is much more. And it's personal.

Getting Started

I think the best way to get started is to list the words that describe your company. There are lots of lists you can find on the internet to assist. You can have a marketing firm direct the project. Or you can start with your own list of adjectives. To help, I think you need to assemble a team of people whom you trust and respect within your organization. People who are honest and thoughtful. Brainstorm with the team, pick the words, then put them in context. We did the exercise at my company, CK and CO, and here are a few of our findings.

> **Fun:** There's never a dull moment at CK and CO! We're a group of fun, upbeat, and, yes, usually noisy people who care deeply about each other. We produce great stories because we trust and always look out for one another and our clients.

> **Bold:** At CK and CO, we are bold. We go above and beyond for our clients, doing things no one thought possible, even under ridiculous time deadlines. We don't back down from a challenge. That's why we consistently deliver high-impact products.

> **Professional:** The production team at CK and CO defines "professional," exceeding client expectations at every opportunity.

Other words that bubbled to the top of our list were: dynamic, polished, one-of-a-kind. When you do this exercise, the words and statements begin to shape your story and the brand voice of your company. It is who you are at the core. What I hope you see is that the words paint a picture and influence how your customers and employees look at and respond to you. One other thing to consider is the tone. At my company, we are by no means "corporate." That why we say things like:

> Don't let our size fool you. We're nimble, dynamic, and clever. And our award-winning work holds up against any big-city

agency with a big name (you know what we mean . . . and who we're talking about).

Some might think that sounds like we are bragging. We are not. We are proud to be a smaller firm that works with big global giants.

What obstacles? We're fierce and yet friendly, especially when it comes to breaking down barriers, making the complex simple, and capturing your story.

Some might think that we foolishly ignore danger. Not so. We simply think we are at our best when we're challenged to do something we've never done before.

John Kowalski, owner of Integrative Marketing Fusion, believes that brand is what precedes you and it can create a market advantage. Kowalski says, "After all, if you've done as outlined above in assembling a list of adjectives or brand assets, they are true to your organization and *only* your organization. To expand on this, a strong brand

- cannot be copied,
- endures hardships,
- inspires,
- is extendable,
- motivates,
- creates loyalty, and
- precedes you in every selling situation."[1]

Determine Your Tone

There is a difference between voice and tone. Voice, as we have described, is about your personality. Tone is about emotion. What is your tone? If you are unsure, a good place to start is by looking at the work of the Neilson Norman Group. They have done extensive research and developed the

"Four Dimensions of Tone of Voice." On their site, you can map out where you stand. The four are:

- ▸ Formal vs. casual
- ▸ Serious vs. funny
- ▸ Respectful vs. irreverent
- ▸ Matter-of-fact vs. enthusiastic[2]

Finding your company voice does not need to be complicated, but it *is* work. Once you find it, you need to have a consistent voice in everything you do. That includes your website, social media, emails, recruitment ads, face-to-face meetings, campaigns—everything you do to communicate.

Find Your Voice, Step by Step

First, write it down. **Document the work** you did to find the words and statements that define you. Put it into a comprehensive report. Make sure everyone understands the work and knows where to access it. Communicate it. This is who we are. This is what we stand for. This is where we're going. Make it clear for everyone. Create a brand guide—what you can and cannot do with the logo, colors, fonts, and formatting. People in your organization may resist sticking to the standards. Hold firm. Don't let anyone mess with your brand.

Second, **train communication champions or storytellers.** Don't assume that leaders are able to communicate to their teams and employees. People need to be trained how to tell your story, taught presentation skills, and given tools to support them. It's important that everyone is consistent with your brand but knows that they should use their own words. People make or break businesses, and their unique personalities and experiences help make the culture and the brand.

Third, **audit internal and external communications.** Are they on brand? What communication vehicles are you using and what is missing? What tools are you using to create communications? How frequently do you communicate? It's easy to be consistent when you first start, but things can get off track quickly. Be watchful.

John Kowalski shared a great exercise that he does with every new client. He has them assemble every piece of literature or tool that has the logo on it. That includes everything from marketing brochures and customer quote forms to installation instructions and finance forms. But he goes even further. Kowalski says:

> What about electronic elements? PDFs, email signatures, and website assets. Everything. Then I have them scatter around a large table and ask, "Do these things look like they come from the same place? Do they communicate the words and statements that define you?" If so, great; if not, you're off strategy and need to work on some cleanup. I refer to this as a brand audit but at the highest level.[3]

If everything is not consistent with your brand, how can you expect potential customers to know and appreciate who you are and what you stand for? Kowalski also says that some of the most important things to consider during an audit may not be as obvious. That's why he creates a laundry list of everything that "touches" a customer.

> Look at things like trucks and building signage. Name tags. How does the receptionist greet guests? How does a service technician in the field behave? All these elements must help support and build your brand. It's a long-term process that takes years and consistency. And when you really invest in a branding initiative, it's important to not only have leadership behind *you* but also everyone within the organization. Everyone can be a brand ambassador, carry your message, and help others get on board. The more the merrier.[4]

Fourth, **keep working.** Things change, and you need to review and revise your work. For one thing, language changes, as does the meaning of words. You don't want to sound out of touch or "old." I have not mentioned visuals, but they are important in telling a company story and can also become outdated easily. As your organization changes, as technology and innovation progress, make sure your written content, imagery, and video reflect and hold strong to those brand words or assets you developed.

One note of caution. Sometimes there is a push to change things too quickly. Not because there is a reason, but just for the sake of change. John Kowalski has seen this time and time again.

I've had leadership ask after six months, "Okay, what's next? We need a new campaign; I'm tired of this one." That is a very fair statement, but it is flawed. Not only are you building your brand from the inside out, but it is also external. Internally, people may have seen your brand refresh a thousand times. That's great, but your external stakeholders and customers may have only seen it twice. It takes an average of seven to nine times for a consistent message to embed itself within someone's head. So keep the campaign running for much longer than your gut says it should continue. The focus is on the external audience, and changing perceptions takes time—a long time. Keep at it. For a brand initiative, there'd better be a good reason for a change, adjustment, or refresh.[5]

One last thing to consider. Finding your company voice and maintaining it can be tricky, especially for start-ups. You wear many "hats" as you build a customer base and secure and maintain funding. And as you expand your organization, add locations, and grow in complexity, you might need more help. Don't hesitate to bring in professionals to assist. No matter where you are in the life cycle of your business, doing the work to develop a strong company voice helps you build your team and drive more business. We will discuss how this work pays off when we explore how to create brand fanatics in chapter 16.

TIPS TO SUCCEED

▶ Company voice is important. Do the work to define it.

▶ Your company should have a personality. Make a list of the words that describe it.

▶ Determine if you can do this work on your own or if you need outside help.

12
CLIENTS AND EMPLOYEES: WHEN TO LOVE THEM AND WHEN TO LEAVE THEM

t's a fact—growing your business with existing clients is much easier than getting new ones. But sometimes you need to take stock of the customer base and see if you still love them, or if it's time to leave them.

When you first start out, you're tempted to take whatever business comes through the door. Sometimes, it's a customer you don't really want or is one that's not well suited to your core capabilities. For example, one of my clients wanted us to do car commercials. Yes, those cheesy ones with the owner of the dealership on camera touting a big, once-in-a-lifetime sale. At first, we did these really awful TV spots. Let's face it; even projects you hate pay the bills. But these small-scale projects were labor and time intensive, and often not very profitable. As I started to study the composition of my client base, I found there were a number of things to consider, including whether I needed to leave or send them away. Here are some points you might want to consider, as well.

First, the work! Is the job something that fits well into the existing work-flow, processes, and capabilities of your company? Would it be a stretch to deliver what your customer is asking for or require a capital investment that you are not prepared to make, like adding inventory? What if it just isn't work that you are ramped up to do? If the work is not part of your core capabilities, it will take longer to accomplish, and you will get distracted from your base business. I'm not saying that you should just do the "same old, same old," but you also need to think about whether the client can, and will, be good for your business in the long term.

The next thing to consider is the quality of the work that the client is asking you to do. Those cheesy car commercials did not do much for the reputation of my business in the early years. If someone were looking at those spots as an example of our work, they did not reflect our ability or the quality that we could deliver; not to mention that what you attract is often more of what you already have. This was not the kind of business that I wanted, so I did the unthinkable and made a list of all the clients that we needed to get rid of. I also started to look through our client base to identify those who brought us the kind of work we wanted to do, work that would reflect well on the company and help us attract big new clients. It worked—thirty-five years later, our client list matches the kind of work we are good at and want to do.

Assess the Value of What You Provide

Every so often, you find a client that you just can't please. You make a recommendation, and they fight it, or they simply ignore it. They tell you exactly what they want, you produce it or do it, and they don't like it. But they blame you for the results. They don't provide the information you need to do the job in a timely manner, but they still expect you to deliver on time. It's one thing to run into a snag on a project or get surprised by something that is out of their control. When that happens, we spring into action and do what a good partner does: we deliver. However, when these types of situations become the norm, then it is time to assess the value of the relationship. The hassle factor may be too great to continue with them.

Another point to consider is the constant pressure to lower your price or their refusal to pay for things that are outside the scope of a project or changes that they requested. In the product area, where costs are on a per unit basis, customers use the lure of big volume to try to negotiate a lower price. This is a common occurrence, and while sometimes there is a value to offering a discount, often it puts your company in a difficult position.

Here's just one example. Butterball Farms, Inc., is the largest national dairy supplier of specialty butter and premium butter in the US, but it is still a small company. CEO Mark Peters decided to take a calculated risk with a large customer. Here is how he describes what happened:

> We worked on a project for about a year with a company where we did the research and development and the flavor profiles. We were very up-front about the cost of the product all the way through the whole process. We did samples, and we put a lot of money into it over the course of a year. Then, six weeks before product launch, they came and they said, "The pricing isn't going to work. You're going to have to lower your pricing by like fifteen cents a pound." That was all of the margin in the product.[1]

Peters went on to say that they simply were not going to lower the price. What ensued was not very pleasant. He told his chief operating officer to call the customer, take him out for lunch, and just say that they had no interest in doing business with their company. As Peters describes it, the reaction of their customer was interesting: "He said, 'Well, don't you even want to negotiate this?' I said no. You know, we found out what kind of character that company had, and I decided the best time to say no to them was before we were reliant on their revenue."[2] Peters said the other company took the research and development and produced the product internally. Interestingly enough, they didn't do it very well; about a year later, they came back to Butterball through a broker, and Butterball ended up making the product after all. Peters let his customer walk away, but they came back.

This story illustrates a point that needs to be emphasized. When you start to feel like you are getting beat up on price, you need to take a good, hard look. Are you competitive? Will dropping the price seriously impact the financial health of your company? Will you start to resent the customer, and will that have an impact on the quality of the relationship or on the product? If you answered yes to some or all of these questions, then it is time to rethink your position.

How to Leave Your Clients Gracefully

Of course, getting clients to leave is not exactly fun or easy to do. You need to be systematic and thoughtful. You can't send a lot of clients away at once or you'll face another problem: cash flow. When we decided to take stock of our customers and really focus on the ones we loved, we started by identifying our biggest problem clients. Truthfully, there were not many. That surprised us, but if you think about it, it makes sense. It only takes one child misbehaving in a classroom to change the environment. One difficult client can do the same. It makes your employees anxious, disrupts the work, and just colors everything. We planned our strategy for when we would ease clients out and how we would communicate with them.

For the most part, I think the clients understood. I told them that we were moving in a different direction and thought that they would be better served by a different type of production company. I identified a couple of options for companies that could help them and passed along their names. If you are going to send clients away, there is one thing to note: don't just cut off service or product flow; help them make the transition. You never know—there might come a time when you want to welcome them back.

By sending clients away, I had more time to seek out and develop the kind of business that would position the company to move forward with the effort to attract bigger businesses from all over the country. In all honesty, it took a while, but it was well worth the effort. Of course, if I had been a little more choosy at the outset, then I wouldn't have created the situation. So, think clearly about the customers you want and don't be afraid to turn those away who don't meet the profile. Then, work like crazy to get the kind of clients you do want.

When Clients Want to Leave You

Of course, it's important to be prepared for when a client wants to leave *you*. It's bound to happen. No matter how good you are, or how long you have worked with a customer, the day may come when one of them just wants to try someone or something new. This is especially likely to happen if you own a service business or if a good contact leaves a company and is replaced by someone who wants to bring in their own preferred suppliers. What do you do?

This is the time to be very careful. For a number of years, we produced a year-end communication for a client. When we contacted them one year to start the work, the marketing director told me that they decided to try something different with another company—I was shocked. There was no sign that they were unhappy or even looking to find another supplier. I tried to find out the reason for the switch. I asked a few open-ended questions and just got polite, vague responses, so I did the best I could to respond. I told the client that I completely understood and that sometimes it's good to try something a little different. I also added that I hoped if they ever needed anything, they would feel comfortable giving us a call.

It took an entire year, but the client did call us again. It seems that the "something different" they tried did not work out. While I did not probe to find out the details, over time they let enough slip through that I knew they did not have a good experience, had paid more, and did not feel that the new supplier had lived up to their promises.

Customers We Love

While I have spent a lot of time talking about leaving customers, it is also important that we address the customers we love. These folks are easy to spot. They appreciate your efforts, they tell others about you, they send you flowers—really. (I thought it was supposed to be the other way around.) They apologize when they ask you to do something that they know is difficult. They include you in discussions about their plans so you don't get surprised by things that may impact their relationship with you, whether that is a change in their buying habits or their expectations from you as a supplier. These are customers who care about your business and want to be sure that you are successful. They are true partners.

One example of a true partner is Bradford White. Headquartered in Ambler, Pennsylvania, it is an American-owned manufacturer. The company is known for its residential, commercial, and industrial products for water heating, space heating, combination heating, and storage applications. From the time we began working with them, it was obvious that this company cares. When changes occur within the company, they alert us. We don't need to read it in the news. As we work on projects, they are open and honest. They want us to be able to do our best work. As opportunities arise for us to stretch our capabilities, they give us the green light. When they come to town or we visit them, we are treated like part of the family.

This caring also extends to their network of builders, contractors, professionals, and wholesalers. They provide education, training, and support. This is a client that you "love." That is not to say there won't be problems. Client relationships are complicated even under the best circumstances, but when you find clients that you love, protect the relationship. It is invaluable.

Show Your Appreciation

How do you show your customers that you appreciate their business? Say it every chance you get. Send them an actual thank-you note, not just an email. Try to accommodate them when they have an urgent need, and don't make it sound like you are doing them a big favor. Understand that they have bad days, too, and need your support. If appropriate, invite them to events that might appeal to them: a concert, the theater, a charity gala. One thing that my company likes to do is to feature customers in our video newsletter. This is a terrific way to put the focus on them. If you have a blog, you can use that communication to promote them or causes that are dear to them. You might also feature them in a print ad. Just remember, however, that it is always good to run any of this type of activity by them first, as some of your customers may not want the publicity or attention.

There are companies that routinely hold customer-appreciation activities. It's not just one event or a gift to a client; it is a carefully thought-out experience that shows customers how important they are to the business. That can be anything from a small intimate cocktail party for those who want to just stop by and visit, to inviting a group to the theater or a sporting event. If you sponsor a community event where the proceeds go to nonprofit agencies, you can invite customers to attend with you.

Think about it. If you are spending your time with customers who are holding you back from the work you want to do, work that will move you closer to the customers you want to attract, take the difficult action to leave them. And, when the relationship is good for everyone, make sure you show your appreciation. Smart owners know when it is time to love clients and when it is time to leave them.

Time for Employees to Go

Just as there is a time for clients to "go," there is a time when you need to show employees the door. Conventional wisdom says to attract and retain good talent. That has been increasingly difficult in recent times. Competition for employees is out of control. That has put pressure on employers to create a better work environment, offer incentives and perks. The list of well-known companies that provide sometimes amazing perks is lengthy—everything from a free on-site fitness center or hair salon to massage therapy and cash bonuses. But is this realistic for a small business? Should you encourage employees to move on from time to time and bring in individuals with fresh ideas to help you better compete? As you attract bigger businesses, can your employees handle more complex interactions?

Over the years, I have come to believe that there are times when you should encourage employees to move on. This is especially critical for small businesses because employees do not have as much opportunity to "move up." As a result, they get comfortable. They often quit trying to excel. They get stale. I have seen this happen time and time again.

Perhaps the most obvious case of this in my business was a young woman who began working for the company when we were just a two-person operation. At the time, the company was located on the top floor of a building that had an art store below. For a while, "Mary" was a wonderful employee—responsive, attentive, and organized. But as our organization grew, she did not. She became annoyed as we tried to expand our client base and attract bigger and more complex customers. She became more sensitive to any type of constructive criticism.

It all came to a head when we moved from our humble offices to our own beautifully remodeled building. The new offices were modern, had lots of style, and were certainly more reflective of our high-tech business. From the time we started planning the move, it was obvious that Mary was not happy. She refused to assist with the move and never adjusted. She became combative with fellow employees and terse with clients. Why? Perhaps she simply did not like change. Maybe she was more comfortable in a smaller business, dealing with less sophisticated clients. Who knows for sure? What I did know was that it was past time for her to go. I had missed the opportunity to respond to the red flags that appeared over a lengthy period of time. In the end, I fired her.

This is perhaps the most difficult decision that every business owner has to face. You want to have a solid staff. You do not want to keep training new employees. You want to show a consistent face to the customer. But if you work with an employee, remove barriers, provide them with opportunity and reasonable development, and there still is not enough progress, then you have to let them go. If you don't, the collateral damage to the organization can be great.

In another case, I hired an individual as a producer. During the interview process, he was personable, outgoing, and appeared to have the necessary skills. However, several months into the job, it became clear that "Kevin" was not who he had appeared to be. He had managed to put up a good front but could not sustain it day to day. He was quiet, reserved, and very much a loner—a huge problem when you work for a communication company.

I encouraged him to be more outgoing and modeled how to interact with customers. In the end, he simply did not have the personality to do the job. Several customers told me it was painful trying to have a conversation with him. When I sat down to tell him that I was terminating his employment, I think he was relieved. Kevin was not a good fit for our organization.

Since Kevin and Mary left, our organization has progressed and grown. Change is good. The individuals that filled those positions have taken us much further and instituted many new ideas. The business has benefited from their fresh eyes and fresh thinking.

Is It Time to Go?

In many ways, this is all about alignment. Think about what happens when your spine is out of place. You go to the chiropractor because everything hurts, you can't be productive, and the work you do is not very good. You get an alignment, and everything starts working again. The same is true of organizations. When your organization is out of alignment because employees have not grown and changed to fit a new reality, the business can't be efficient or grow. Here are a few questions to ask to help determine if it is time for employees to go:

- Is the employee stuck or ineffective because of something that you have done?
- Have the working conditions changed, and they simply cannot adapt?
- Is the employee not being challenged or not challenging themself?
- Are your customers making comments about the lack of service, poor quality of product, and attitude of the individual?
- Is the individual damaging the culture of the organization?
- Is the individual's attitude affecting the morale of your other employees?
- What is the cost of keeping them?
- Can you replace the skill set?

You Made a Bad Hire. Now What?

Here is one more thing to think about: perhaps the employee was simply a bad hire from the start. If you discover that, even after all of your best efforts, the employee is not right for your company, don't prolong the inevitable. Take a little time and do a short assessment so that you can have a clear conscience. Ask yourself:

- Were the expectations of the job clear, and did you communicate them?
- Did you provide performance feedback and coaching?
- Did you give the individual all the training and development necessary to be successful? Sometimes people derail themselves. They just don't want to be successful.
- Have you removed barriers and provided opportunity and reasonable development without seeing any progress?

If you answered yes to even one of these questions, then I think it is time to take bold action quickly. It will save you much heartache later. Yes, you should try to attract and retain good employees, you should take care of employees and mentor them, and you should help them to grow professionally. But when there is no opportunity for them to move up, help them move on. When they simply can't perform and are never going to get there, don't just fire them. Treat them with respect, talk to them, and gracefully move them out. Besides the altruistic reason for helping a struggling employee move on, it's also practical. Yes, it will save paying unemployment but, perhaps most importantly, it also helps maintain good morale and loyalty with your remaining employees.

Employees You Love

The employees you love are the ones who "get it." I have staff that have been with me for over twenty years. I don't know if I am smart or just lucky, but these individuals work at a high level, both professionally and emotionally. They treat customers as I would. They go out of their way to make things easy for me and their fellow workers. They love what they do. These employees will do anything they can, and they don't compete with each other. They know we are all on the same team.

So how do you show these employees you care? Give them the ability to make decisions. Teach them all you know. Offer as many opportunities to grow as possible. When they make a mistake, take the blame. You don't need instructions to spot these employees. You do need to watch how they operate and acknowledge their good work. And show them some love. Send them home early on a Friday to be with family. Have a movie day. Go golfing. Do a community project together.

A Few Final Thoughts

Customers and employees can influence how much you love or hate your work. The good ones keep you getting out of bed every day, eager and excited to go to work. The bad ones are like a constant headache. Choose wisely when to love them and when to leave them. If you do, you and your business will be healthier.

TIPS TO SUCCEED

- ▸ Develop a profile of your ideal customer and your ideal employee.
- ▸ Identify the steps to leave difficult customers and employees gracefully.
- ▸ Create a plan to replace that business or employee.
- ▸ Show your customers and employees how much you appreciate them in interesting and creative ways.

SUCCEED AT GROWTH

13
PAY ATTENTION TO SMALL CUSTOMERS— THEY CAN GET BIGGER

Every business owner dreams of landing the big one, the customer or project that catapults their business to the next level. That's why business books on the best-sellers lists have catchy titles, usually about the big score. *Whale Hunting* by Tom Searcy and Barbara Weaver Smith, for example, provides a step-by-step guide for how to land big sales and transform a company. But taking on small projects or customers, the ones your competitors won't bother with, can also reap big benefits and have a large, long-term effect on your business.

For example, one day the phone rang at our office. The caller was a marketing director at a small subsidiary of a global manufacturing company. He was looking for someone to take a PowerPoint presentation and turn it into a short video with narration. Not a big job and not a big budget.

I started to ask questions: "How did he find out about us? Had he done video before?" That's when it got interesting. He explained that the company did have a current supplier; they had worked on a number of projects to date with fairly large budgets. However, this time that supplier was not interested in the work. They had told him this job was too small. They only took on big-budget, higher-profile projects. The marketing director was frustrated and annoyed because the video was part of a presentation to secure new business. It was supposed be that little extra something to help differentiate his company from the competition. The turnaround was tight, and he did not really have time to look for a new supplier. I agreed to meet with him early the next week.

When I arrived, I did not jump right into details of the project; instead, I asked if I could tour the facility. He looked surprised that I wanted to spend the time, considering the size of the budget. I explained, "I always like to have more information than I need to do a project." He obliged and took me on an extensive tour of the plant, showroom, and offices. It was very obvious that he was proud of the place and that there could be huge opportunities if they could secure this new business.

When we finally sat down to discuss the project, I did not proceed to show him how we could do what he was asking. Instead, I offered some ideas to make the video more impactful. Why not feature the team who would be working on the project and make it more personal? How about shooting some additional video to entice the potential customer to come and visit? I explained how we could change the scope of the project and still stay within the budget.

It became obvious to my new client that I would devote the time and attention he needed to get this done. After it was complete, he began to send other projects our way—bigger ones. One day, he alerted us that the parent company was looking for a supplier to produce an ongoing communication. He got us on the Request for Proposal list. We responded and showed examples of our work, including the pieces we had created for the subsidiary. Because of our experience, and coaching from this marketing director, we won the contract. That first, simple $2,500 project opened the door.

The lesson is clear. Don't judge a potential opportunity by the size of the budget. Pay attention to what can happen when you help someone and deliver more than they expect. There are countless examples like these of companies that simply would not take the time because the project was too small, not high profile, or just not exciting. There are also examples of start-up companies that no one wanted to service. Great little companies with interesting or niche products can take off. If you pay attention to them while they are small, you might just have a big customer for life.

Grow as Your Customer Grows

Marilyn D. Landis is president of Basic Business Concepts, Inc., and a former board chair of the National Small Business Association. Her multi-faceted service firm provides support to keep businesses financially on track and growing. Some clients use her firm as their CFO instead of having a full-time CFO on staff. Landis also provides financial consulting services and more. But not everyone needs, or can pay for, what she provides. Landis created a "Help Desk" for these individuals who operate early stage companies that are not that complicated yet. Landis says:

> The reason a help desk works for a new entrepreneur is the built-in learning opportunity. We all learn best when we are learning for a reason. Founding, growing, and thriving as a new entrepreneur is a powerful reason. The passion that drives an entrepreneur to take the risk is what will make their business uniquely competitive. Instructing them, suggesting what information they need to research, test, and organize into a plan for their business, channels that entrepreneurial passion into knowledge. As they gain that knowledge, they ask better questions. We find that cycle gives them powerful insights into not only their business but their industry and their market segment. We don't have the knowledge they have of their business space, but the "help desk" gives them the benefit of our experience as to what questions to ask and how to mitigate risk.[1]

The beauty of this model is that young entrepreneurs get an experienced advisor and can access them as needed. Landis is providing what smaller customers need today and will be there to provide more sophisticated services in the future. In the end, as her clients grow, her business grows. Paying attention to small customers makes good business sense.

Are You Ignoring People Who Have the Real Power?

You also need to pay attention to and look carefully at your contacts within the organizations you serve. Many business owners believe that they need to work directly with top management and ignore those with positions that may not seem influential. That is a big mistake. Here's just one example.

The marketing director at a company we serve had the opportunity to hire a number of individuals to support the field sales department. One individual was a young man with good experience and a lot of ambition. At first, he was managing smaller projects. Our team worked with him and provided the same high level of creativity, quality, and service that we would for much bigger projects.

The young man worked hard, got noticed, and was given more responsibilities; he excelled. The parent company of our client tapped this young man for a professional development program that would put him in line for bigger opportunities. It did not take long. He accepted a position with the parent company at the corporate headquarters. I stayed in touch and was delighted to see how quickly his career was progressing.

One day, he called: Would I take the time to talk through a potential project with some of his colleagues? He was clear that he was asking for a favor. They already had strong connections to a company that would probably get the job. They just did not want to tip their hand about the budget or show that they were not as savvy as they should have been about buying this service. As a favor, and not expecting any business from the call, I obliged. Shortly after, I received a Request for Proposal. I was surprised to see that the RFP contained all the things I had coached them to do. Needless to say, we bid and won the entire contract. This company has become a major client for our business, and we travel throughout the country to this day to work for them.

Sometimes the individuals who can help you the most have what appears to be a lower-level position. Stop right there; I know what you are thinking: they are just a project manager, administrative assistant, or receptionist. I figured out a long time ago that these are the individuals who are quietly influencing others around them, and their managers rely on them to do lots of research to help them make decisions.

For instance, one day I was scheduled to do a seminar on how to present more effectively at a logistics company. I arrived early, and the receptionist told me that the room was not yet available. Instead of sitting down and ignoring the woman, I engaged her. I asked questions about the company and what she liked about working there. We had a delightful conversation until I was able to go in. Shortly before my presentation started, I noticed that the CEO had entered the room and sat down in the back. I had not met him prior to that day but had seen his picture on their website. I was surprised, since he had not been scheduled to attend.

The presentation went well and afterward he came up to introduce himself. I asked why he had attended, and his response was, "Mary at the front desk called me and said, 'You've got to meet this girl.' I wasn't really planning on staying for the whole presentation, but I really enjoyed it." I went on to get a number of additional jobs from this company—all because I paid attention to a "small player."

It's tempting to only target big customers or projects. It's easy to disregard individuals whom you believe are not in a position to send business your way, but smaller customers and individuals in middle management positions can be as important to your business in the long term. That's not to say that big business, or high-level executives, aren't important to our bottom line. Our larger customers have been a tremendous source of referrals. But starting out with smaller customers and projects allows you to get to know their business and prove yourself. And it is nice to have a mix of clients at various stages of business, from start-ups to second-stage and beyond.

Relationships Matter

It's easy to say that relationships matter. After all, who can deny that people do business with people. Our large customers have been great at promoting us. They have opened the doors for us at trade shows and introduced us to their suppliers and customers. At times, they have pointed us to others in their industry that have needs. Recently, I got a call from an out-of-state company. I wondered how they had found us. When I asked, the individual said, "My boss was at an industry conference and the subject of video production came up. One of the other attendees said if you need video, call CK and CO, they are the best. When my boss came home, he told me to find you." To this day, I don't *know* who recommended us, although I can guess. We now have a new client.

Another example of how these relationships impact your company is much more personal. Today's employment situation is fluid. People have options about where to work, how to work, and with whom they work. I have seen a great deal of movement as people consider these options. Some have been with a company for many years and decide to leave. They want to try something new, don't see the possibility of progressing where they are, or have personal reasons. Not to mention the fact that some get poached by competitors or customers who have seen their work and want to recruit them.

When you develop a close working relationship with someone, and they understand your value, they open doors at their new company. I have at least a half dozen customers that we have worked with at more than one company. They move, we get a new client. It is truly a win-win. They know that we will deliver for them because we have done it in the past. They also know we want them to succeed and appreciate the introduction. We get access to a whole new book of business and grow our top line.

One Company, Big Connections

One of the easiest ways to develop new business is to look at smaller companies and see if they are a part of a larger organization. Often, large companies break their business into smaller divisions or business units. Get into one, and you get into their procurement system. There is no doubt that it is not easy; however, once in the system, you get calls from a variety of places. And, if you develop a relationship with a procurement person, they can recommend you to others. But don't just wait for the business—ask.

If you are working with a smaller business unit, see if they will get you a simple "meet and greet" with others. It doesn't need to be related to a specific project, product, or service. Just a short meeting to explain what you do and "plant a seed." Then stay in touch. It may take a while, but if you are in it for the long haul, it is worth it.

TIPS TO SUCCEED

- Look for small companies that have interesting products or services and are poised for growth. When you build a relationship with a small customer and they grow, you do too.

- The individual with power may not always appear to be influential.

- Think of yourself as an extension of your customer's organization, not just a supplier.

- When a company is part of a larger organization, try to make connections with the other parts.

14
THE BIG BUSINESS BUYER'S PERSPECTIVE

F or a number of years, my company has been working with Siemens Corporation, Cisco Technologies, and other large global firms. The relationships have been good. They have helped me to understand the buying process in more detail and connected me with other large companies. I want to share some different perspectives on working with big companies.

Years ago, I wrote a book entitled *Small Business for Big Thinkers: Unconventional Strategies to Connect with and Win Big Business.* At that time, I interviewed Carl Oberland, who was the vice president of supply chain management, North America Region, for Siemens Corporation. He told me then, and I still believe to this day, that there is a difference between the service-focused small business and the manufacturing products–focused business. At the time he said:

> If you're in a pure services side of the business, to my way of thinking, it's a bit easier to do business with big companies. That's because the smaller service company is largely selling people's individual competencies, capabilities, and the ability to match up culturally to the big company client. In addition, the flexibility and the ability to tailor the offering to what the client needs exactly may be easier on the small business side than it is in a big player's house. If the players

on a small company team have the right competence, expertise, and experience, then the buying company will not have any reticence to engage.[1]

So that is the service side of working with big business. How about on the manufacturing side? One of the issues here is the ability of small business to stay technologically up to date. I believe that bigger manufacturing companies plan and budget for research and development, as well as property, plant, and equipment improvements. That is key! Today, customers are looking to see if smaller firms have adopted Industry 4.0. Have they worked to digitize their business or are they still doing things the "old-fashioned way"? The Industry 4.0 initiative was designed to help manufacturers—with a strategy, digital technologies, and understanding the data that can help solve challenges. A smaller player may have a plant that looks modern, but buyers want to know if you are able to stay on top of technological developments over time the way a bigger player can.

Ultimately, purchasing organizations must evaluate both services-based small businesses and manufacturing-based small businesses as to their business sustainability. This refers to the ability of the business to sustain itself over the longer term. If the small businesses are selling people expertise, then the risk that must be evaluated is whether the business has a fallback plan if key personnel leave the company. If the small business is manufacturing, and has special intellectual property or patents, then the risk is whether access to this technology will continue to be available to the purchasing company if the small business has a major business interruption.

The pandemic also made buyers much more concerned about the ability of smaller companies to manage disruptions in their supply chain. Those who were creative and resilient did well, but many did not.

One area where small manufacturing companies can compete effectively is the production of niche products that big companies need but may not want to manufacture. Take, for example, the case of Butterball Farms, Inc. CEO Mark Peters works with some of the biggest names in fast-food chains, as well as major food producers. Says Peters:

Our relationship with a major producer of butter is kind of interesting because big companies really struggle with doing niche products. They have their center-of-the-bell-curve product lines, but they always want to have a leading-edge product. They may want a product that's got a higher margin, or that's not price competitive. The problem is that this is not their core competency. They're not good at making it. So, we've sort of defined this market. If it's a product that is under fifteen million pounds a year, that's a small market for a large company. But we play really, really well in that space. We can take a product like that, from test to national scale, and do the whole thing.[2]

The type of business is one of the pieces of the equation. The second part of the equation is the whole financial picture, which comes into play for both services-offering companies and products-and-solution companies. Most large companies will do a Dun and Bradstreet report and also ask a potential supplier for a financial statement. This is important because it provides them a good picture of your financial stability—your receivables, inventory, and how your business is faring from a cash-flow perspective. This is critical because no customer, large or small, wants to have you come to them partway through a project and say, "I can't go on and finish this unless you loan me some money."

This is a challenge for smaller players who may be unprepared for the ninety-day payment terms that are standard for larger companies. I can also attest to the fact that we have had many issues with larger companies when people leave and have not submitted our invoices. It has taken me up to a year to get some of them paid. If cash flow is a concern, you might want to see if your customer has a supplier-financing program. You discount your receivable a bit, but you often get paid in ten days or less. Many suppliers have signed up for this type of financing program so that some of the cash-flow issues can be overcome.

In this regard, my customer, Siemens Industry, has been innovative. Other large corporations have experimented with this type of supplier-financing program. For many years, I did not take advantage of this program. It was not until my procurement contact reached out one day and asked why we were not enrolled. Since we had good cash flow, I just fig-ured we did not need it. I was wrong. Even if you have good cash flow, this is a great program. One other point to note, it is not just smaller compa-nies that take advantage of this program. Even big firms are utilizing it.

The truth is that small businesses need to understand the position of big business. Carl Oberland described it this way when I spoke to him many years ago:

> Think of our responsibility as a triangle. There is the financial side, the quality side, and the delivery side. And the quality and delivery do affect the financial piece. We'll call the financial piece the initial price. It is important that small businesses are able to articulate their ability to satisfy all three corners of that triangle because it isn't always just about price. They need to be able to emphasize their ability to deliver on time, with a quality solution or quality offering.[3]

To broaden this perspective beyond my customer base, I went searching to find another buyer with diverse experience in global purchasing. Chris-topher Locke has been in the industry for forty-five years, with nearly half that time in global procurement. Having negotiated and sourced billions of dollars' worth of diverse products and services for companies like Chrysler Corporation, Rolls-Royce Power Systems, Albemarle Chemical, and Hertz Equipment Rental, Christopher is presently the executive vice president of strategic sourcing at Centerline Publishing & Consulting. Over the past twenty years, he has written articles and given presentations regarding "the sales process from the buyer's perspective" for organizations such as the Association for Manufacturing Technology, the Michigan Minority Sup-plier Development Council, and the National Association of Women Busi-ness Owners. He is also the acclaimed author of *FEEDBACK: Sales Advice from the Buyer's Desk* (available only on Amazon), the only sales book writ-ten by a professional buyer.

Locke has some very definite ideas about the advantages and disad-vantages of doing business with small and large businesses. Some of this is based on fact and some of it is perception. And, of course, it certainly does not apply 100 percent of the time.

The Advantages of Working with Large Companies

First, let's look at the advantages of choosing a big business as a supplier. According to Locke:

> The perception is that a big business is more financially stable and less likely to close their doors. They have more diverse products and services and can provide them nationally, even globally, to all of my facilities. If I only had one facility in one state, that would be one thing, but I have facilities all over the world. Smaller companies may not be able to meet my needs for products and services at all of my locations, much less provide service, maintenance, repair, or sales representation.[4]

Locke goes on to say that larger companies have more complex research-and-development facilities, which often provide a technological advantage that smaller companies simply do not have. Says Locke:

> In our mind, larger companies are more organized. Why? Because they have more specialized departments in quality, specifications, research and development, manufacturing, and sales engineering. If you deal with a smaller company, they may not have a good comprehension of what we are looking for simply because they don't have anyone who has the time to read all of the specifications. They just agree to it without fully understanding it. Larger companies are also more likely to be certified to the most updated industry standards. At least that's our perception.[5]

The Disadvantages of Working with Large Companies

If this sounds like Locke is biased toward large companies, he is not. He says larger companies also have many disadvantages. Larger companies have a less personal relationship with their customers because they have so many clients. They are also less likely to accept the preferred contractual terms and conditions, including payment terms. Larger companies are slower to respond to emails and voice mails. Locke says, "They also have a higher rate of turnover when it comes to sales representation. I'm working closely with someone for three months, then he or she is reassigned, and someone else takes over the account who knows absolutely nothing about my company or what we've been working on."[6]

Locke agrees with others that he is not likely to be dealing with executive management at a large company, and certainly not the CEO. The highest level he might be able to reach is the sales manager, and usually not someone who can make things happen. It is just a fact of life that there is more red tape and bureaucracy in dealing with large companies as suppliers. Locke goes on to say that sometimes larger suppliers simply do not want his business and shares this story:

> I was talking with a few of the buyers at our company, and one told me he received an email that a supplier had mistakenly passed on to him. In it, the supplier said that they didn't even want our business because they felt we were not buying enough from them, or that the profit margin wasn't high enough. So, they would rather not work with us at all.[7]

According to Locke, that is rarely the case with a smaller supplier.

The Advantages and Disadvantages of Working with Small Suppliers

What are the advantages and disadvantages of working with a smaller supplier? Locke says that smaller suppliers are more willing to ship product or deliver services before receiving payment or even a purchase order. In urgent cases, smaller companies understand that products are needed as soon as possible so that work can continue without shutting down the line. I can attest to this point personally. I often have large customers call with last-minute requests. I never hesitate to respond because I know that I will get paid. And I know this because I have a close, personal relationship with the customer. In thirty-five years, I have not been disappointed. So another advantage—a close, personal relationship—is one that almost every person I spoke with mentioned. Locke says:

> Smaller suppliers will spend more time with me because they have a few key customers. Smaller companies are also more willing to accept our purchase order terms and conditions. They have faster response times with emails and voice mails, as well as delivery of product. I am also able to communicate directly with the owner or the CEO of the company when I need to get things done. I can even show up at their door without an appointment to check on my project. You simply can't do that with a big company supplier.[8]

The disadvantages of working with a small supplier have been previously mentioned, but here are a few additional points. Small suppliers are more likely to close their doors because of cash-flow issues. They may not have global representation. The loss of one big client can have a significant impact on a small business. It is often the case that small suppliers become very dependent on a few big customers and literally stop their sales efforts.

Do Small Businesses Get Special Treatment?

You may wonder if smaller suppliers get a break because they are small or if the expectations are the same no matter what the size of the company. It depends on the situation. I can tell you from my own experience that larger companies may be willing to register you in their system and make some accommodation. For example, we have made the case that we do not need to carry the same insurance as larger firms because of the type of work we do. We have also successfully lobbied that we did not need some certifications that were part of larger companies' standard requirements. I think larger companies understand that there are some things that small businesses just can't do, specifically in the financial area, simply because we are small. But I do think that we need to be able to compete to win the business, and that might mean doing some of the things that are required for all businesses.

Trends in Buying

No matter the size of the company, there are a number of buying trends that all businesses should note.

Consolidating the Supply Base

For many years, there has been a movement to reduce or consolidate a company's supply base. That makes sense. Why would you buy parts from ten suppliers when you can buy from two and reduce the amount of paperwork and effort, not to mention reduced costs based on higher volumes?

But given the disruption in the marketplace, inflation, and protectionism, many are rethinking their approach. Businesses are looking to develop a strong, resilient stable of businesses upon which they can rely. According to the EY Industrial Supply Chain Survey, "Changes to supplier bases are even more prevalent: 62% of respondents said their companies have made significant changes in this area in the last 24 months, and 55% say they are planning significant changes in the next 24 months. For these companies, increased diversification and proximity to their customers are key outcomes."[9]

Respondents also said they are increasing their total number of suppliers and are shifting their supplier footprint to be closer to their operations and their customers. That may bode well for small businesses who are ready to compete. For some companies, it is not big versus small but rather a focus on certain *types* of businesses. That may include minority, woman-owned, veteran-owned, or some other designated status. A good idea is to do your homework. Check out the philosophy of the potential client. Read their corporate responsibility initiatives and see if they align with your business. While some companies want to do business with a certain type of supplier, say smaller companies, they may not have a lot of time to go looking. *You* will need to find *them*.

Cost Savings

A second trend is cost savings. Here, Christopher Locke is careful to point out a few facts:

> For me, it is not about beating a supplier up to get another dime out of them. It's about best value. It's about working smarter. It's about

the buyer asking the supplier, "What can we do to save money? What specifications are we asking you to adhere to that are costing us money needlessly?"[10]

There are some companies that believe in early supplier involvement. They are looking for the supplier to innovate and bring their know-how into the process very early on in the design phase. Usually, this type of early involvement is used more in areas that are not considered a commodity. For example, you don't need early supplier involvement in buying staples. But you might need it if you were designing a new type of engine or a new marketing campaign.

If you can bring this type of expertise to a customer and help them design a new product at a lower cost, you will be considered very valuable.

Faster Delivery

Another trend that I have personally experienced is the need to do things faster. Projects that used to take six weeks to complete are now due in two to three weeks. The delivery of products also has a compressed time frame. Let's face it, we have all gotten used to the fact that we can go online, order something, and it shows up the next day. As consumers, we are demanding and always looking for a new and improved product. As a small business, you must be able to respond to that if you want to maintain and grow.

Global Cooperation

An important trend to note is the closer cooperation among buyers' global counterparts. Today, buyers share information with the buyer sitting next to them and with those around the world. When Locke was a buyer, he said:

> I communicate with my global counterparts. We're sharing information about the projects we are working on, the products we need to buy, and who we may want to buy from. Then we go to the supplier and tell them that we're interested in having them quote one thousand widgets for me, two thousand for the buyer in Germany, and five thousand for the buyer in Japan. We tell them that it's critical that they bundle the widgets to provide cost savings to each of us. We are also looking further out. We might have five projects in five different countries with five different buyers. We need to know what

kind of cost saving each buyer can realize if the supplier gets all five of the projects.[11]

TIPS TO SUCCEED

▸ Suppliers, big or small, are evaluated on the quality of their product or service, ability to deliver, and the value they provide, not just the price they bring to the customer.

▸ There are advantages and disadvantages for both the big and small supplier.

▸ Ask about corporate goals.

▸ Many large companies may have aggressive payment terms, so be prepared for how that might affect your cash flow. Some companies do offer a supplier financing program.

▸ Buyers share information with their global counterparts, so you may need to be able to provide goods and services around the world.

15

RFPs, SOWs: WHAT IT TAKES TO COMPETE

R FI. RFP. RFQ. SOW. It is a bit like alphabet soup, but you need to know what the acronyms stand for and, more importantly, how to respond or walk away.

Request for Information

Let's start with the Request for Information, or RFI. Think of this as a fishing expedition. The buyer is just casting a net to see what is out there. The buyer wants to get a general idea of your business and is looking to see what potential suppliers might be able to provide. The information is not binding nor any type of formal quote—it is *just* information. The buyer might send certain Requests for Proposal your way based on what you provide.

Request for Proposal

The RFP, or Request for Proposal—also known as the RFQ, or Request for Quote—is enough to send small-business owners running for more familiar selling situations. I almost did not respond to the first RFP I received because it seemed like a massive amount of work, and the level of detail requested was unbelievable.

I did not understand some of the terminology or acronyms. Big businesses love to use terms that you can't even Google because some of them are specific to that individual company. In addition, it seemed like I would have to guess or make projections about things that I would not be able to control. Finally, all the legal language about "failure to deliver" made my eyes cross. Quite honestly, I thought it was scary. I am embarrassed to say this, but the first time I responded to an RFP, I did not read all the requirements in the small print. Today I know better.

What do you do when you get one of those complicated RFPs or RFQs? Ask questions and spend lots of time putting together your response. I got over my fear, I did the best I could, and we got the job. We did business with them for thirty years until they created an internal department.

There are a couple of things to note when you start to respond to Requests for Quotes. First, let's look at the buyers. Individuals who create RFPs may or may not be experts in purchasing those types of goods or services. Perhaps the purchaser is really good at buying raw materials but does not understand how to buy training services. Very large companies do have buyers with what they call "category experience." This means that, in addition to a college education—whether it is in finance, engineering, or business—the buyer has a deep understanding of how a particular industry works. Maybe they know material handling, or plastics, or glass. Or the buyer may have acquired the expertise to buy a particular product or service over time.

Many companies have boilerplate language inserted into every RFP, even if it does not have anything to do with what is being requested. It can be confusing, and you have to wade through all of it or you might miss something. Through the years, I have learned a lot about how to respond.

For example, don't wait too long before sitting down to read the often-massive document. If you do, you may not have enough time to devote to your response. In the past few years, I have seen companies send out RFPs with very large opportunities and a very short time frame to respond to the request. I wonder if that is part of the strategy of the business: to see if the potential supplier can respond intelligently and quickly to the RFP. That may or may not be the case, but sometimes it feels that way. If you start early, you will have time to gather all your questions and get them answered.

Reading and Responding to the RFP or RFQ

Most Requests for Proposal have a number of different types of information, some of which may be helpful in framing your response. In a typical RFP, you will find:

- Table of contents.

- Background on the company, including its website.

- Description of the project and deliverables. You may be asked to respond to the entire project or given the opportunity to respond in part.

- Scope of responsibilities: what will they provide and what are you expected to do?

- Proposal development and work schedule with specific dates, when they need a response, when the project will be awarded, when the work must begin, and when you need to deliver. There might also be milestones that you need to reach.

- Specification requirements for what they need.

- Change requests and how billing is handled.

You should also be ready to provide detailed information about your company, including:

- Your company's geographic reach.

- Your company's capabilities.

- Use of subcontractors or freelancers. It is really important to note why you are using these individuals, how they will interface with your team, and your past experiences with them.

- Financial statements or information.

- Description of projects you have done that are similar in nature to the project on which you are bidding.

- Your approach to the project and how you will ensure a quality product and on-time delivery.

- ▶ Samples of your work or product.

- ▶ References, certifications, and, of course, pricing.

Pay special attention to the individual who is making the request. You can usually submit questions to that person to help you develop a response. Think like a student: go through and highlight everyplace where you have a question so you can submit all of them at one time. If you ask intelligent questions, you start to stand out from the others who are responding. Look for gaps in the proposal and make suggestions for how they can be addressed. This may impress them and help to open a dialogue with individuals who can assist you later in the process. It is a chance for you to show them how interested you are in the company and the project. I like to map out or group the information. Here's how I do it.

WHAT DO I KNOW ABOUT THE COMPANY?

I like to find out about a company from research I do on my own, not just from the RFP. What is their style: formal, informal, conservative, or cutting-edge? Can I find someone who works there who can give me insight? Ask around; you might find that people you know do business with them already, or they might know people who work there.

WHAT DO I KNOW ABOUT THE PROJECT?

Why are they putting this project out to bid? Is it something they cannot or do not want to do in-house? Is this a new project or product? Are they trying to find a new supplier to replace one that is not performing? Is this a high-risk project? Is this something that is highly technical and has not been done before? Will this require research and development for you, or is it right in your wheelhouse? Is the timeline reasonable? All of this helps you understand their hot buttons. You can then use that information to write a dynamic response that is extremely targeted to what is most important to them.

WHAT DO I KNOW ABOUT POTENTIAL COMPETITORS WHO MAY BE BIDDING?

This one can be a little tricky. Here's a tip: look at the location of the company's headquarters and other major facilities. Now use the internet to search for your competitors in that region. Check their websites and see if they refer to the company that sent out the RFP. Many times, you will find your potential competitors. However, competitors are not always those who are in direct competition with you; they may be businesses in related industries, companies that are looking to expand into your area.

Doing research will help to differentiate yourself so that you have the strongest positioning possible. One other thing to note: by doing research, you may find that the RFP is just an attempt to get a current supplier to be more competitive or that the RFP is really just a formality, and you probably do not have a chance of winning it. In that case, you might want to pass and use your efforts to go after business that you do have a chance of winning.

WHAT DO I WANT THEM TO KNOW ABOUT MY COMPANY?

Small businesses tend to want to tell a potential customer everything there is to know about them, including boring historical data. Resist the temptation to do that. You need to provide what is essential for the RFP reviewer to know—that gets you to a physical face-to-face or virtual interview.

Start by looking at existing proposals or marketing documents that you have already written, especially those that have won business in the past. Can some of this be repurposed or targeted for this RFP? Don't reinvent yourself; look at what you have, build on it, and customize it. What are the unique capabilities that make you a good fit for this opportunity? Do not sound like every other company; find something about you and your company that has the "wow factor" and use that.

Try to give examples of specific experiences that show you have done this type of work in the past. If you don't have something that correlates exactly, show how your experience in other situations applies here. For example, a plastics manufacturer asked us for a proposal to create a communication about a proprietary process that they believed would help them win business with an automotive manufacturer. We had never done any work in plastics, and I was not familiar with extrusion machines. But I did know a lot about manufacturing, and I discovered that they participated in lean manufacturing. This model is based upon the Toyota Production System and is all about removing waste and becoming efficient. We had worked with a number of manufacturers that were lean, and I had even read a number of books on the subject. I leveraged that experience in the proposal, and we won it.

HOW DO I ESTABLISH PRICING?

This one is difficult, especially if you are in a service business. If you are providing a product, you know the cost of raw materials, labor, the margin you need, and the like. The same, however, does not hold true for services. Is an hour of your time worth more or less than an hour purchased from the competition? That depends on the level of expertise, but, as a starting point, I recommend you do extensive research to see how your initial pricing compares to other firms in your region and across the country.

This is not as tough as you might think. In fact, at one time we simply called companies and introduced ourselves. We did not try to covertly get information; we were honest in saying that we wanted to do benchmarking of our pricing. Most were incredibly open once they looked us up on the internet and found out that we were legitimate. Many of my customers have told me that price is important, but they will pay more for something if the supplier can demonstrate the value of their product or service. Of course, you still have to be competitive.

Large companies often have an idea of what they believe a project or product is worth before they send out an RFP. The trick is to figure out that number and if it is realistic for you. I call it the magic number, but, actually, it is more like a range. Price is always a consideration, but I have won many contracts where my price was higher. How did I do that? I educated the buyer about the value of working with us. I showed them how we ensure quality and create communications that have shelf life, so that they don't need to create a new video year after year. I showed them how we archive their assets, so they are available for future projects. Bottom line, we might cost a little more, but they get more and achieve a better outcome.

Christopher Locke, a Certified Professional in Supply Management (CPSM), uses this simple example to illustrate the point. He is going to buy pencils and asks three companies to submit bids:

> If it is my perception that every pencil is exactly the same, I would be stupid not to pick the best price. But if the supplier educates me about his pencil, that his pencil is the only one that has an eraser, so I won't have to go out and buy that separately, then I realize it's not an apples-to-apples comparison like I thought. Most suppliers

complain that it's all about the price. But if the supplier does not educate me about his product, then price is all I have to go by.[1]

If you are doing a significant amount of business with a company, they may want to put you on a master service agreement. That means you have to give them your very best pricing and guarantee it for the length of the project or a period of time. How much you discount is a delicate decision. Discount too much, and you put yourself at risk; discount too little, and you may not be competitive. It's an art. One thing to remember is that many potential big-business clients are willing to pay your price if you have value-added services or faster response times.

One final note on the structure of the response: do not get creative. My experience is that big companies prefer you to respond to each section and label it clearly. It helps them compare responses without having to search for information. It also helps them to see that you have provided all of the requested information.

Using a Scope of Work

As an option, some companies use a Scope of Work (SOW) document for new or current suppliers to understand a project and generate a quote. A Scope of Work is a little different from an RFP. It contains a high-level description of the goals, milestones, stakeholders, costs, and approvals. Sometimes the SOW will be very detailed if the purchaser knows exactly what they want. Other times, the Scope of Work is purposely vague. Here, the purchaser is looking to see if you are creative, innovative in your approach, and able to think through the project and produce fresh ideas.

John Kowalski puts it this way:

> I look to see if the person responding to my SOW was really listening. Do they get what I am trying to achieve, and do they really want to work on this project? I am looking for something beyond the same old thing. I can get that from a big company. There are times when a small company can come up with ideas that I have not even thought about, and that's what is great about working with a smaller firm. They make my project better and I will gladly even pay more for it when they put in the time to create something truly unique.[2]

Get Creative

In addition to having a complete response, you want it to stand out. This will help you get short-listed, so you actually get some face time with the potential client to make your case. In this situation, you can think creatively when crafting a response to an RFP or SOW. For example, when we responded to an RFP for a Wiley Publishing's *For Dummies* project, we wrote it in the style of these well-known, step-by-step books. I summed up the background section on my company, Cynthia Kay and Company, by saying in "dummies language," we hope you will:

1. Use the highly committed media professionals of CK and CO.

2. Put CK and CO's technology to work for you.

3. Have CK and CO create concise, friendly presentations for "Dummies."

We also printed the response to the RFP and had it bound so that it was an actual book. Yes, it was more expensive, but it was worth it. We got a contract and have been working with them since 2009.

In other cases, we have produced videos to accompany our response to RFPs. If you go this route, it is a chance to put your people front and center. Let them tell the potential client how they will serve them, how they ensure quality, and why they believe they can do the best job. It does not have to be highly produced, but the quality does need to be good, and the people must be believable. You can also ask current customers to provide testimonials.

If video isn't your thing, you can create an add-on print piece. Take photos of your employees or customers and use short, powerful comments that endorse your company or show why employees are excited about the project. Make it visually appealing.

Other techniques might include sending clutter busters. These are objects or samples that stand out from the typical ones, anything that will get attention and get you noticed. The cleverer you are, the better, but be careful that you do not go too far, or it might backfire.

If you do the hard work of putting an RFP together and don't make the cut, don't despair. You will be able to use parts and pieces for the next attempt. You should also see if the buyer will give you constructive feedback about why you did not get the job. Some buyers will not return your request for information. But I have had great conversations after the fact with buyers who have helped me shape future RFPs.

You Got Short-Listed. Now What?

If you get the chance to meet in person, don't waste the opportunity. As Christopher Locke says:

> This is your chance to get your foot in the door and do business. This is the most important meeting of your life as far as my company is concerned. Unfortunately, most potential suppliers come in with a generic presentation, the same one they use on every company and on every department within that company. I am not just any company. I am not just any department. I am a buyer, and I have different wants, needs, responsibilities, and goals than other companies and other departments. Sell to me based on who I am, because so much of what is presented is not anything I want or need to hear. That is a waste of my time. Then, when I ask a question like "What are your preferred terms and conditions?" they can't give me an answer. Good luck getting another meeting with me.[3]

TIPS TO SUCCEED

- ▶ Figure out how to connect with likely targets and get on a list for RFPs or SOWs.

- ▶ Spend time reading RFPs carefully. There is a lot of critical information that can be buried among all the legalese.

- ▶ Break the needed information into sections and tackle them one at a time.

- ▶ Be sure that the information you present is customized to the opportunity. Don't use a generic approach.

- ▶ You may only get one chance at a face-to-face meeting. Be prepared to answer all the questions.

16

CREATE BRAND FANATICS AND NURTURE THEM

H ave you ever had someone tell you about a new product and literally gush? The person goes on and on about how they love this product, how great it tastes, how wonderful it is to use. You get the idea. They almost sound like they are getting paid to promote the product. This is what I call a "brand fanatic." A person who had such a wonderful experience that they can't help but tell other people. These people will wear your hats and t-shirts. They will sing your praises to anyone they can. And some, think Harley Davidson, even get logos tattooed. Brand fanatics are your biggest champions.

Alfie Logo Gear designs, creates, and produces logo gear, branded merchandise, and creative solutions for companies, teams, events, and organizations. Alfie has an amazing way of doing business and has lots of fans across the country. I am one of them. I asked CEO Bonnie Alfonso for her definition of a brand fanatic. "A brand fanatic is an ambassador and advocates for your company. You are *the* person and your company, your organization, your brand is who they think of immediately when they need what you provide."[1]

So, you might wonder how you create brand fanatics? I learned early on that to get anyone excited about your brand, you must excel at your work. You must love your work, and people need to see that. One day, I went out to a customer site to do an interview with a product manager. The company was launching enhancements to a product line that was old and tired. The video was supposed to get the sales staff educated and excited about this relaunch.

When I walked in the door, I saw a man standing at the reception desk. Before I could even sign in, he greeted me and said he was my interview. He hustled me down the hall, talking all the way. He said he was so excited to meet me. Others had told him that working with me was "an experience." I asked the obvious. A good one or a bad one? Fortunately, a good one. He went on to say that others had said how easy it was to work with me, that I had coached them and made them look good on camera. I evidently had several brand fanatics at this company.

To create a brand fanatic takes time and effort. According to John Kowalski, owner of Integrated Marketing Fusion, it comes down to the value that you provide—not once but consistently.

> Number one, to turn someone into a brand loyalist or a brand fanatic, you really need to solve a problem for them. You need to alleviate the stress that they're dealing with day in and day out. If you can do that, it is a huge relief for them. Number two, it makes them look good within their organization and to their leadership. You are propelling that person's career forward. In return, they are loyal and bring you repeat business.[2]

This idea of creating value and solving a problem is echoed by Bonnie Alfonso. She believes in being a resource for her clients. It is not about just making a sale or completing a transaction. It goes much deeper. Alfonso says:

> The focus is on being a partner and creating a relationship. If I can be of service and provide gear that complements the work and culture of the organization, it is an honor. Approaching opportunities with a "How can I help?" mind-set changes the energy and experience.[3]

Make Connections. Delight Customers.

I had a client many years ago who taught me about the idea of delighting the customer. Honestly, when I first heard that, it sounded a little cheesy. Really, delight them? That was until I started to observe what it meant. For example, if this client quoted a delivery time of three weeks, they tried to deliver in two. You might not think that is a big thing, but customers really were delighted that their product was showing up early. They also communicated more than just the typical confirmation of order and shipping. There are lots of touch points where you can build excitement about your product or service and help the customer experience your brand.

Alfie Logo Gear is thoughtful about every opportunity to wow the customer. It is not one thing but a series of small actions that make the difference. Alfonso says:

> People come to us because they are proud of their company, organization, or team and want to share it with their employees, clients, and community. Logo gear helps build connections. The little things matter in building connections: state your name when you answer the phone, include your contact info on all emails—both of these little actions convey that you are welcoming, engaged, and available. Seems obvious, but it is often overlooked. Then there are bigger things. Keep your word, set realistic expectations of what you are capable of and the timeline, and then follow through.[4]

Don't Just Perform, Overperform

I learned long ago that just doing the job is not enough. You must overperform, go beyond what someone asks, think with them and sometimes for them. Here is one example. A number of years ago, we responded to a Request for Proposal. There was a contact name for questions. After thoroughly reading the RFP, I developed a series of questions about what was needed, including a few questions that pointed out some significant gaps that might cause issues in the delivery of the product. I emailed and asked if we could chat.

The conversation started out in a very formal tone. But as it continued, it became obvious to the buyer that what I was asking could help her streamline the project and even cut some costs. I also found out that the company had previously contracted for this type of work and had been disappointed. The project was over budget and had poor results. She had been burned and did not intend for that to happen again. We responded and won the contract. Then we made this buyer look good. We delivered ahead of schedule and on budget. We had our brand fanatic. When another project surfaced, she alerted us that the RFP was coming and had a very tight turnaround for the response. She also provided guidance on what had been budgeted. That was valuable information that helped us frame a response that was appropriate for what they wanted to spend.

A brand fanatic is important because in many companies there are so many pockets of business that you, as an outsider, simply can't find them all. A fanatic recommends you to their colleagues, gives you information about what is important to the company, and maybe even gets you on a preferred supplier list.

A Brand Champion or Two

You should also seriously consider cultivating a number of champions at a company because businesses are constantly shifting people around. Therefore, it is likely that today's champion may not be in a position to help you tomorrow. You can minimize this particular risk by working to develop relationships at various levels of the company.

Mark Peters, CEO of Butterball Farms, Inc., takes a slightly different approach to the idea of having more than one champion. He says:

> I literally had an "aha moment" years ago listening to a presentation on negotiating with big companies. When you go into a sales presentation with a big company, there is rarely any one person at a table who can say "yes." But if anyone at the table says "no," that one person can kill the relationship. You don't need all of them to be advocates. You need one or two of them. Try to figure out the person in your organization who matches up best with key individuals in their organization. It might be the purchasing department; it might be the quality department; it might be the distribution department. You need somebody at that table to say, "I love working with that company, and it's going to cost us a lot if we switch or don't hire them." It's different with different customers, but you need to find that key connection point. And it could be in a number of areas.[5]

Pull Out All the Stops

When you do make it onto that list or get that job, you must make your champion look good. That means everything from pulling out all the stops to delivering something on a ridiculous timetable. Suggest process improvements. Figure out how to help customers with tight budgets. Here are three examples of pulling out the stops.

Example 1: Use Creative Tactics

John Kowalski has worked in a variety of industries and has great examples that illustrate how to get attention with creative tactics.

> When I worked at a major office furniture manufacturer, we typically set up furniture for the potential customers' staff to review and give input to decision-makers. It is called a "mock-up," and I worked with the sales team to present our best foot forward. For a mock-up at a beer manufacturer, we had six-packs of their bottles wrapped with our features and benefits on custom bottle labels. The bottles got so much attention at the facility that individuals were walking over three quarters of a mile in the plant just to see them.

> Another mock-up was for a nature-television network. We created woodland elements within our products. We hung customer banners to create a backdrop to the furniture. We created a "journey" map as they viewed the furniture. Going the extra mile when your competitors don't builds your brand. Listening to customer challenges while your competitors talk about their features and benefits builds the relationship. You are there to solve a problem, and in doing so, you can make an acquaintance a brand champion for life.[6]

Example 2: Make It Easy for Clients

Bonnie Alfonso knows that companies love their own logo and brand and want merchandise that reflects that. But the person in charge of purchasing the gear may dread being a "personal shopper" for all of the employees. Alfonso decided to go above and beyond and make it easy. Alfonso said:

> We implemented a company portal process that streamlined employee purchasing. After meeting with the client and creating a wish list of

their gear, we provide virtual proofs and begin building their own custom Company Store. We field all team member questions, process the transactions, and produce the gear. When our team packages the order, we envision the experience of our client and work to save them time and make it efficient. The items are neatly folded and individually packaged. We want to make it seamless for the person that is responsible for ordering the gear and distributing it so they are excited, and willing, to do it again. Plus, they look like a rockstar.[7]

Example 3: Think Beyond Ordinary

At CK and CO, we are used to last-minute calls from clients. So we were not surprised when a client got short-listed and had an opportunity to win a massive global contract. They needed help to put together an RFP that would really stand out. I could have just created something based on their information, but I really wanted to help this brand champion because they were taking a chance on working with us in a new and different way.

I started to think about how I might get inside information that would be valuable. I combed through my contacts and came across someone who used to do business with my client's potential client. I made a call and asked if he still had contacts who might be able to help. The answer was yes. In fact, there was a recently retired executive who might provide information. I wrote a list of questions, and we got the answers. We developed a very nontraditional, creative presentation that really wowed my customer's potential customer. They got the global contract, and I got another brand champion who told the story of how we had helped him to many others in the company.

In another case, a potential client came to us for help with the rollout of a new employee-discipline program. We helped them revise the plan and think through the consequences of the timetable, which would involve diverse groups of employees, within the same facility, operating under different rules. We helped them figure out a way to streamline the process. As a result, they looked like heroes to upper management. By the way, we did not take credit for the work. By making your brand champion look good, you deepen the relationship and generally win more business.

One more thing: when looking to find and nurture brand fanatics, don't discount those who do not have a title or seem to be big players. As I mentioned in chapter 13, you might be surprised. Sometimes the champion is the quiet influencer behind the scenes. Think about the executive assistant, the project manager, the store clerk, the receptionist. They all know things that you need to know if you want to get into a company and grow the business. Most of them are happy to share information with someone who is authentic about their intentions, respectful of their time, and truly grateful for their efforts. Go find yourself a champion or two, and watch what happens.

TIPS TO SUCCEED

- To turn someone into a brand loyalist or a brand fanatic, you need to solve a problem for them.

- Try to identify individuals who can provide you with information and be your champion. It might be a behind-the-scenes player.

- If at all possible, have a number of individuals in different areas to help you make connections.

- Pull out all the stops to make your champion look good; they got you in the door and can keep the business coming.

17
TECHNOLOGY: FRIEND OR FOE

I look around and see so many opportunities for businesses to use technology. Salesforce (a cloud-based software company), handheld devices, and ordering systems are just a few examples. Frankly, I am at a loss when people say they don't love technology. I believe that if technology is not your friend, doing business in today's world is difficult, if not impossible. Technology has permeated every single aspect of our business world—from hiring new employees and using platforms like Indeed to ordering systems, invoicing systems, and CRM (customer relationship management) systems. Technology is what fuels a business's efficiency.

I know some say, "My business is too small. My business is not that complicated." The truth is that even simple operations benefit from the use of technology. If you are not using technology, it is likely that you are missing out on gaining a host of efficiencies. My sister, who is only a few years older than me, did not like technology. She would be the first one to proudly tell you that she ran a multimillion-dollar company using a flip phone. But she is the exception, not the rule. For most people, that would be impossible.

Most of my customers require that we submit all proposals and invoices online. Some have their own portals, others use Ariba or similar systems. If we want to work with them, we must learn to use these systems. It is not always easy, but to do otherwise is not an option. And because we have made it easy for customers to do business with us, we get more projects and referrals.

Budgeting for IT

While some businesses are good at budgeting for people and equipment, many struggle with an IT budget. In fact, most have no budget at all, and IT ends up becoming a constant unplanned expense. There is no doubt that it is tricky for smaller companies with twenty or fewer employees to decide what to spend and where to spend it. One way is to allocate a dollar number per person. There is no hard-and-fast rule for what that dollar number is, but Chad Paalman, CEO and cofounder of NuWave Technology Partners and a member of Cisco's managed IT service provider (MSP) advisory board, said, "small businesses should look to spend about 6 percent or more of gross revenue."[1] Paalman goes on to note six things that go into planning an IT budget.

1. **The cost to implement and maintain your foundation network infrastructure.** This includes internet and phone service, firewall, routers, network switches, wireless, and end-user devices such as computers, tablets, etc.

2. **Decide if your office and productivity files will be stored on local servers or in the cloud.** More and more IT services are moving from a one-time capital acquisition model to a monthly "as a service" model. "Cloud" services are a good example of this. Simply put, the cloud refers to a network of remote servers that are used to store, manage, and process data over the internet instead of on a local server or personal computer. Both Microsoft and Google have pushed users of their product suites to the cloud. Although Microsoft does still offer on-premises options, most organizations over the past few years have determined that a cloud-hosted option works best for them.

3. **The cost to implement line-of-business applications.** Many industries have applications that are specific to business; for example, CPAs, attorneys, or manufacturing operations. Most of these applications, like the office and productivity applications, have moved from being hosted on on-premise servers to the cloud.

4. **Cybersecurity is an ever-changing and evolving area of IT.** In addition to the cat-and-mouse game of staying one step ahead of the

bad guys, cyber liability insurance and/or regulatory compliance is drastically increasing the investment in cybersecurity for many businesses. Over the past couple of years, the cost of maintaining cyber liability policies has increased significantly. As a result, businesses must continually increase their investments in cybersecurity and add new tools such as multifactor authentication (MFA), endpoint detection and response (EDR), security information and event management (SIEM), etc.

5. **Support for remote workers** is not necessarily a new topic. However, many businesses now have some or even all of their staff working remotely. To ensure adequate security and to provide maximum productivity, many businesses have significantly increased their investment around support for remote workers.

6. Last, but certainly not least, **who is going to support your IT?** Smaller companies typically outsource their IT to a managed service provider (MSP). Midsize and larger companies typically have an internal IT person or department, and many of these still leverage an MSP to augment their staff.[2]

According to Payscale, the 2023 yearly national average for a network administrator is a little over $64,000,[3] whereas Glassdoor indicates it could be nearly $80,000.[4] According to Paalman, the industry average for an MSP is $150 per person per month for companies with twenty to one hundred employees. Paalman noted that companies with regulatory compliance requirements are paying upwards of $300 per person per month or more!

Options for Managing IT

So where do you start? As the old saying goes, "You don't know what you don't know." That is especially true when it comes to technology. There are several options to consider. As Paalman suggested, I tried having an in-house IT person and soon discovered that did not work. To begin, the cost of having that person on the payroll did not match the benefit. Additionally, one person cannot be an expert in all areas. On top of that, most business owners do not have enough knowledge of IT systems to know how to manage an internal IT person.

If you want someone on staff, consider a co-managed program where your internal IT person supports your end users, and you partner with an outside IT firm/MSP that assists in supporting your overall network and cybersecurity. The option I prefer is a fully managed program. Just as you might hire an outside HR team to work with your company, an outside IT firm can save you money, make recommendations, and be on call for 24/7 support. How do you choose? Rely on the experts and know that the decision may change as your organization changes.

The best way to find the IT support you need is to ask others. How do you find an attorney or CPA? Chances are that it is through word of mouth. That is a good place to start, but then look at the IT company's sweet spot. For example, some want to service organizations with fifty or more users. Others concentrate on smaller firms. There are IT companies that specialize in certain industries such as healthcare, defense, or manufacturing. Ask questions. And be aware that you need to proceed with caution when selecting a firm. Chad Paalman explains:

> Here's the dirty secret of the IT industry. It is an unregulated industry. There is no licensure and no regulation to operate. So anybody—unlike a CPA, attorney, or most other professions—anybody can throw up a shingle, which can make it very difficult to compare MSPs. Ask for references! There are certifications out there. CompTIA is the big one, and there are manufacturer certifications. However, just because you have industry certifications, such as CompTIA, or manufacturer certifications, such as Cisco and Microsoft, doesn't mean that the IT company knows what they are doing or that they have stayed current.[5]

Bottom line. Do your homework. Is the company that you are looking at just trying to sell you "block dollars" for service? A good IT company will suggest starting with a third-party assessment from a firm that does not actually provide you with IT support. That type of company is not trying to win your business, so they can provide an unbiased opinion. They evaluate your technology infrastructure, review your applications, your policies, and procedures. This is an area where many smaller organizations are lacking.

Consider an Assessment

An assessment can expose weaknesses such as outdated equipment, applications that are no longer supported, and vulnerabilities. It can also inform decisions and uncover opportunities to use technology to automate some tasks, reduce manual work, and increase accuracy, as well as help you stay compliant. Once you find a third-party firm, ask what cybersecurity framework (CSF) will be used to do the assessment.

Many IT professionals like to use the NIST CSF. The National Institute of Standards and Technology (NIST) is a federal agency that is part of the US Department of Commerce.[6] It is a world leader in the development of cybersecurity standards and best practices, so their framework can offer information and activities that companies can put into practice quickly. One thing to note: an assessment is not something you do once. It is a constant effort, and the frequency is dictated by how quickly your industry and business experiences change.

The question is not do you *need* technology but what *types* of technology and how will you manage it? One of the biggest issues with smaller organizations is that they add technology in pieces rather than taking a wholistic approach. This is another area where an outside firm can assist. IT firms can make recommendations and help you build a technology plan and budget that directly aligns with your company's goals. Today it seems like just about everything is connected to the internet. Your IT company can assist with network infrastructure, cloud services, and help you find the right tools for collaboration. This is becoming more important as people become more mobile and need to work anywhere and everywhere.

What to Expect from Your IT Company

It can be difficult to know if you are getting the most from your IT dollars. What can you expect from a reputable managed IT firm? First, look at communication. Are you getting regular reports that show the health of your system? Do you see how they have resolved issues? How responsive are they when you call for support? Chad Paalman says that you should have a review process either monthly or quarterly.

We call them strategic business reviews. It is sitting down on a regular cadence saying, "Here is what is new. Here is where you have gaps." I think a managed IT company owes it to their customers to provide them with a technology plan and a budget that are aligned to the goals and strategic plans of the business. IT is often seen as a black hole of expense. A properly prepared and maintained technology plan and budget should eliminate most of those unplanned or unforeseen IT expenses.

Today nearly every business initiative involves IT. I tell my clients that I need to understand where you want to take your company so that I can more accurately build a technology plan and budget that aligns to your business goals. I need to know what is your one-, two-, three-year plan. Are you going to add people? Are you adding locations? Are you adding new service lines? So, as you are building your plan of what you are going to do with your business, we help with the corresponding technology expenses to achieve those business goals.[7]

Get Systems in Place

There are two acronyms that are important: CRM and ERP. A customer relationship management (CRM) system is critical for keeping track of potential leads and client information. We use a system that was designed for creative agencies that allows us to track contacts, proposals, projects, costs, and more. It also allows us to generate invoices and interfaces with QuickBooks. It works well for us and is cost effective.

For businesses that manufacture or distribute products, there may be a need for more a robust system. Most modern enterprise resource planning (ERP) systems offer modules that include a CRM, as well as accounting, inventory, HR, and marketing automation. Some systems are free, others have a reasonable monthly subscription, still others are pricey. When it comes to "free" software, Paalman reminds you, "If it is free, you are the product."

There are many pros and cons to using these technology tools. Employees may not have the skills or desire to learn new systems. Implementation can be complicated. Costs can be significant. However, there are also advantages because you get visibility into your operation and can make more informed decisions.

ChatGPT

The buzz around ChatGPT is unbelievable. Don't know what it is? You are not alone. One thing is clear: it will have a significant impact on all businesses. I asked ChatGPT, "How do you explain ChatGPT to someone who has never heard of it?" This was the response:

> Sure, I would be happy to explain ChatGPT to someone who has never heard of it before. ChatGPT is a type of artificial intelligence (AI) language model that has been trained to understand and respond to human language. It works by using a complex neural network that has been trained on a massive dataset of human language, allowing it to generate responses to questions and statements in a way that is natural and conversational.[8]

Not bad for an explanation. So, for example, I could ask it to write this whole section of my book. I did not. However, there are books on Amazon today that have been written by AI. While that is interesting and even amusing, there are so many other areas where ChatGPT can be applied. Let's say you have a service center, and someone files a service ticket. ChatGPT can offer suggestions on how to fix the problem and even help the service tech with suggestions on what to try first—the most likely repair scenario. Lawyers have many tools to find information about cases that set precedents, but some believe this tool can do more. ChatGPT goes beyond and helps "think" through the problem and provide intelligence. There are so many areas that could be impacted.

Of course, there are questions. What should you automate? What should people do? Is ChatGPT good in certain areas but not others? Is the content that ChatGPT creates accurate? What are AI hallucinations? Why does it sometimes generate erroneous content? Will we even need people for tasks that have been automated?

This is an evolving area—one that scares some people and excites others. There is no doubt that ChatGPT is going to change how business gets done and that early adopters will have the edge. But there is also concern that it is moving at a frantic pace and that its impact cannot be predicted. By the time you read this, so much will have taken place. Bottom line: I believe that we will need a number of experts in different areas to help explore when and how to make ChatGPT work for our small businesses. If you want to know more, open a free account at *chat.openai.com.*

Compliance and Cybersecurity

Technology is also critical to ensuring cybersecurity. Your customers want to know that you have taken the proper steps to protect your business and their information. It is a way to retain business or get business. Additionally, there are more and more requirements surrounding compliance and cyber-security, especially in certain industries.

It is a common misconception that small businesses don't need to worry about security. After all, they are small; why would they be targets? The truth is that smaller organizations are at greater risk because they are often easier targets than larger organizations with larger budgets. Smaller businesses may not have the proper safeguards in place or have educated their employees about the dangers. Additionally, everything is now connected to the internet—copy machines, printers, computers, equipment on the plant floor . . . and what about door-access control systems and video surveillance systems. Every device has the potential to be compromised and must be protected.

The term "cybersecurity" is constantly in the news. Chad Paalman offers this broader perspective. Paalman says:

> The industry has talked about cybersecurity for years and years. We talk about cybersecurity, and I joke that the conversations typically focus on building a better fort, a deeper moat around your business. If it was your home, it would be the equivalent of putting on more locks, better deadbolts, adding motion sensors, glass-break detectors, etc.
>
> The challenge is that we need to also be talking about cyber resiliency. It doesn't matter how big your fort is, how many defenses you have put in place, or how much money you have spent on

cybersecurity. Statistically, you are still going to have a cybersecurity event. We need more businesses discussing plans to be *cyber resilient*. Stop thinking *if* you're going to have a cybersecurity event and instead start planning for *when* you have an event and make sure that you have incident response (IR) plans in place. Do you have a plan in place so that you know exactly how you're going to work with your partners, your legal partner, your insurance partner, your IT partner, your crisis communication partner, all those people that are so important to getting you back up and running when you have that event?

In addition to maintaining current offline or air-gapped backups, businesses should also maintain a printed copy of their most important data, including customer lists with contact information, financial statements, and contact information for key contacts such as your attorney, CPA, etc. Most people don't realize that if they are a victim of ransomware—a common cybersecurity threat—their files become encrypted, making them inaccessible. This can include documents, photos, videos, and other important data stored on the affected device or network. This also typically means users have no access to contacts, calendar, or email on their smart phones.[9]

Stories of cyber attacks litter the news, and Verizon's 2022 Data Breach Report warns that small businesses may not survive even one attack.[10] You might wonder why bad actors are ramping up the frequency of attacks. Paalman says:

I answer that question by saying, why do banks get robbed? Banks get robbed because that is where the money is at. The same thing applies here. Threat actors can encrypt your network and hold it for ransom. Maybe you've got trade secrets on your network that threat actors publish on the internet if you don't pay their ransom. There are a variety of reasons; ultimately, data is really the new gold. Instead of robbing banks, modern cyber criminals are robbing businesses for their data, or they're holding your data ransom. It all comes down to the fact that data is the new gold.[11]

For a number of years, I have been on panels with Paalman and other professionals, exploring the various aspects of cybersecurity and the team that is needed to help businesses. Every panel includes an expert in cybersecurity insurance. As we adopt more and more technology, protection is critical. Paalman has this advice:

> The importance of having cyber liability insurance is what the industry calls "risk transfer." If you have an event, you need to have some way to pay for that event. If you have a flood, you have flood insurance. If you have a fire, you have fire insurance. What so many organizations unfortunately haven't realized yet is that, statistically, you are going to have a cybersecurity event. Do you have insurance in place to cover that cybersecurity event? Insurance is needed for a lot of things that business leaders don't think about, such as potentially paying a ransom. It might be to cover bringing in a forensics team. It might just be crisis communications. Do you have somebody that is going to help navigate what you say to the public about this event? It may be to cover the cost of getting your network back up and running. If you have a cyber event, you need help to pay for all those expenses.[12]

One final note. Training is available for end users to learn and stay current on cybersecurity threats. This training is referred to as "security awareness training." According to Paalman, it is critical to continually train and test your users on cybersecurity threats. No one can be fully prepared to deal with the constantly evolving threats, and bad actors are getting more and more sophisticated. Security awareness training, such as KnowBe4, is one resource that Paalman suggests to reduce the risks and avoid human error.

Technology Is a Differentiator

Technology for technology's sake does not make sense. Technology is a tool, and like any other tool, the right technologies, applied appropriately, can be a huge differentiator, especially for small businesses that must compete with larger entities. Technology is your friend, but it also requires that you are open to change and build it into your planning. If you are not willing to spend money to upgrade systems or consistently get support, you will fall behind. If you are not willing to pay for the training so that your people can use these new systems and grow in their business proficiency, then you are at risk of losing them to more advanced companies or having a security incident that puts your business at risk. Technology can be your friend or your foe. You decide which it will be.

TIPS TO SUCCEED

- ▸ Small businesses need technology to help level the playing field. Make sure yours is up to date.

- ▸ There are a number of options for managing IT. Do your homework.

- ▸ ChatGPT is changing the business landscape. See if it could help you.

- ▸ Define a budget for IT that is reasonable for the size and complexity of your organization.

18

HOW TO GET FACE TIME IN A VIRTUAL WORLD AND WHEN TO SHOW UP

Just try to get a meeting with a customer or potential customer. In today's hurry-up, get-it-done, and compressed days, it is next to impossible to get face time in person or virtually. You send emails requesting a meeting, you use snail mail, and you call. The truth is that, until a business has a need or you can create a need, it's difficult—but not impossible—to get in the door. You need to pay very close attention to the opportunities, or you might show up when you don't need to be there or miss a chance to make an important connection.

With more and more business being conducted virtually, face-to-face meetings are rare. One could say that it is the result of limiting the number of people that enter the facility due to safety concerns. That might be true, but why can't you get a virtual meeting? One of the reasons that businesses don't like to meet is that they think you will suck up their time talking about why they should do business with you. Most of the time, they are right. Let's face it. You want to sell them. That's why you may need to change the tone and content of your request.

Our company was doing business with a large firm, but we wanted to do more. Most of my attempts to gain access to the individuals who make buying decisions were largely unsuccessful, so I decided to take a different approach. I looked back over the work we had done and made observations about how we could improve the process and reduce their costs. I talked to a number of individuals and started lobbying for an opportunity to do a short, informational seminar, not a commercial, that would help the product managers and marketers at the company develop and deliver better communications.

At first, I was told that they simply did not let suppliers have that kind of access. I kept trying, and even sent a worksheet showing how a recent project that I had worked on could have been handled more cost effectively. It became clear that I really did have information that would help this business. I got an invitation to speak and flew across the country, at my own expense, to make the presentation. It was two days of traveling, less than twenty-four hours on the ground, and the face time was just an hour and a half. Some people thought I was crazy, or I didn't have enough to do. But it's not about how much time you get; it's about how you use it and what you do to make a lasting impression.

Too often, business owners get stuck doing the same old presentation without really thinking about customizing it or adding the "wow" factor that is needed to secure business. It's like they are on autopilot. In this case, I prepared a "meaty" presentation that was created just for them. I always start with something that is going to surprise them, make them laugh, or get them thinking. You need to grab their attention right away, or you lose them.

I started the presentation by using dramatic examples of how communication missteps had cost companies significant dollars, loss of reputation, and the trust of their customers. The rest of the presentation was designed to help them better understand the topic, the best practices of other large companies, what they needed to do to put a good process in place, and how they could benefit. It was not about my company or our capabilities; it was about their needs. The results were even beyond what I expected. The amount of work they sent our way went up significantly and continues to this day. That is a dramatic example.

There are simpler things, however, that you can do to get face time. I have done significant research to find a potential contact at a company, and I reached out with a very simple request: Can I have fifteen minutes of your time to do "x"? You need to have a hook to get the meeting. Are you going to show them an interesting new technique, a case study that shows how implementing something new can reduce downtime, a demo of something that can improve their productivity? You get the idea. What you are offering is information, a product, or process that is geared toward helping the business solve a problem.

I have also sent out print communications with a call to action. Believe it or not, these actually received more attention than emails because everyone's box is stuffed with spam. In addition, many companies have stopped sending good old-fashioned print mail, so you have less competition for space on the desk of a prospect.

On one occasion, I used a series of six fun and creative postcards highlighting our services. These were highly designed and sent out every other week to large businesses we targeted. It was a mini-campaign to get us noticed, and it worked. This kind of communication can be very effective with companies that are open to using new suppliers but don't want to let you in their door.

Some smaller businesses I know use social media very effectively. Retail, restaurants, and local small businesses that are going direct to consumers can get lots of attention with clever campaigns. However, if your target is a bigger business, I believe they are not as apt to pay attention to you unless they have a very active social media presence as well. They are more likely to rely on other big businesses or partners to find valuable resources.

On the subject of face time, one of the things you need to assess is the accuracy of information from your contact. On more than one occasion, I have had good initial conversations with a potential client but was told there was no need to show up to continue the conversation or discuss the materials I delivered. That's when it's time to really listen and make a judgment about the opportunity. Remember, I said if you are not sensitive to what is happening with the potential client, you might waste your time showing up or miss an important meeting.

Time to Show Up

Does the company have an immediate need, a new product, or a new service? Did they just restructure or merge with another company? Are they dissatisfied with a current supplier? Are they moving into a new area and need the kind of expertise or products you provide? When big changes are happening at big companies, I try to press for a face-to-face meeting, even if it is a brief one. I have driven across town or hundreds of miles; I have flown to both coasts for just a short meet-and-greet.

One potential client said very directly, "I know what you are doing and, really, you don't need to show up. We can just chat over the phone." I showed up anyway, and what I learned by sitting in the room with them was invaluable. It gave me an understanding of the company and showed me areas where we could provide service. I found out why they were walking away from a current supplier. I got a clearer picture of the pressure they were feeling from the higher-ups regarding the need to improve their products. That alone was worth the trip. We won the contract.

When you do show up, you have the chance to deepen the relationship and gain incremental business. I was working on the East Coast for a food company. I took the time to walk down the hall and visit a former client who had changed jobs and was now working for the parent company. All I had intended to do was say a quick hello—that changed. I walked into the middle of a crisis she was having with a project. I spent the rest of the afternoon working with her and picked up a new project and a new client. Was it just luck that I was in the right place at the right time? Perhaps. But if I had not made the effort to connect, I would not have the new client. Think about this the next time you hesitate to show up. What might you be missing?

The time when you absolutely, positively, do need to show up is when there is a crisis or an issue that would be difficult or inappropriate to handle over the phone. When we have a crisis, I am proactive. I don't wait for the client to figure it out; I call them. If we have made a mistake, I tell them— and I tell them how we are going to fix it. If they made a mistake, I still tell them how we're going to fix it. Most companies know that, sooner or later, something will go wrong with a project or a product. "I want to know what went wrong. I don't want to blame someone, but I do want to know how they are going to fix it and what we can learn from this, so it does not happen again. And I want my supplier to be proactive, not just wait for me to call and tell them there is a problem,"[1] says John Kowalski.

When things go wrong, I am amazed at how many business owners handle it by disappearing. I do just the opposite: I barrel in, make no judgments about who was right or wrong, and try to get a plan in place. You can always sort things out later, but showing up to help solve a problem gets you a lot more face time in the future.

One more thing to consider if you are going to show up is *who* should be there. If it is a high-level meeting with executives from the C-suite, don't make the mistake of sending in someone who is not the decision-maker. Don't blow an opportunity to connect at a high level with key contacts. One business owner told me that he did not show up for just such a meeting because it was "only a half hour"—big mistake. Don't confuse the duration of a meeting with its importance; some deals happen very quickly. On the flip side, sometimes you should let others in your organization take the lead. In the case of my company, if the contact is with a highly technical expert, I like to send in my own technical experts. The discussion will be much richer and the connection deeper.

Using Technology to Show Up

Finally, let's talk about when you should consider other ways to communicate besides face to face. For some customers, face time is totally unnecessary. Several of my customers categorically say, "Face time is not important to me. And I don't want to pay the travel costs associated with having someone on site." This is often the case when you work with larger customers who have multiple sites. One customer told me that they value my time as much as they value their own time. It is just as easy to do a phone conference and more efficient. I have successfully used tools like Teams or Zoom, but if you are going to use these methods, you need to understand a few things.

It is easy to do a bad presentation when using these tools because it feels so casual. After all, you are sitting in your own office or location, so it might be just a little too comfortable. You need to create a great professional presence. Find a good background, not the messy part of your office or some dark corner. You can use a nice clean wall, perhaps one that has your company logo on it. Make sure the space does not have many people walking through it or noisy machines, as this will distract you and the others on the call.

Remember to look at the camera, not down at your screen when you are talking. This establishes good eye contact, even though you are miles away. Have a really strong start and finish prepared. Finally, if possible, send materials in advance so that everyone at the other end is prepared, too. If you do it right, they will feel your energy, and you will have saved yourself a trip. If you do it poorly, you will not make a lasting impression, and chances are you won't get any face-to-face meetings.

If your "face time" is just an audio conference, you really have to ramp up your skills. You won't have the benefit of facial cues, and sometimes it is hard to interpret the tone of the conversation. That's because some people are simply not very expressive with their voice. Start by asking who is on the call and introduce others who might be with you. In these types of conversations, you need to listen actively and then use the technique of summarizing what you heard to be sure you have it right.

In today's high-tech world, you need to make the most of all methods of communication. Just being good at what you do, or having the best product or service, is not enough. How you communicate and how much you care about the relationship with your customer make the critical difference. One customer told me, "It's obvious when I am just someone to bill, as opposed to a human being."

TIPS TO SUCCEED

- ▸ Understand when to show up and when to stay home.

- ▸ When things go wrong, don't hide. Show up and be proactive.

- ▸ It's not about how much time you spend; it is about the quality of the interaction.

- ▸ Provide content; don't just sell.

- ▸ Customize the information you present.

- ▸ When appropriate, use technology to substitute for face-to-face communication.

SUCCEED AT STEPPING OUT

19

GIVE SOMETHING AWAY, GET MORE BUSINESS

E veryone likes to get something for free. Just look around, and you'll see businesses that are always running some type of promotion: buy one, get one free; free samples of a product; a free trial membership; a discount through sites like Groupon or Living Social; a free iPad when you buy a flat-screen TV; free software or free information. The practice of giving away something for free has escalated to the point where people expect these freebies without ever thinking about the fact that someone had to design, make, build, and market it.

So, should you consider giving something away as a sound business strategy? It's hard to think about giving away your products or services, but it can actually get you more business and entice customers who might never have thought about doing business with you to try you out. The first thing you need to decide is *what* to give away, the second is *who* to give it to, and the third is *when* to give something away. Let's examine each of these.

What to Give Away

I have seen businesses do giveaway programs that have nothing to do with their business. For example, a furniture store may give away the latest high-tech toy, or passes to the movies, and the like. What's the problem with these types of giveaways? People take advantage of them, get the free stuff, and move on.

I believe a giveaway must be something that is at the very core of your business. This varies dramatically from business to business. Whatever you give away, it has to be of value to the target, or you are wasting your time and money. Can you provide a potential customer with one of your products to try for thirty days? If you are in a service business, perhaps you can provide an initial consultation at no cost? Can you present a miniworkshop or class? Can you do an audit of a business's equipment or technology needs to suggest cost savings? Here's the important thing to remember today, knowledge can set you apart.

In my business, it is not the equipment that sets us apart. Anyone who has enough money can out go and buy the cameras, editing equipment, and software. What sets us apart is the way that we think with customers, the creativity we bring to the project, and the ability to deliver a great product in a very short time frame. We often sit down with a potential client and give them ideas. Some say it's a bad idea to give away your ideas. In fact, there are companies that do charge for their time if they are going to provide what we refer to as creative—that is, concepts or ideas that will be implemented during a project.

When I offer to sit down and think with a potential client, I often get asked, "What will that cost me?" When I tell them that it won't cost them anything, they open their doors. That gives me the chance to show them our interest in their company, the way we work, and a sample or preview of what we can do. It also helps me shape a better response to their project or problem because I have more information. The truth is that it is harder to say no to someone who has taken the time to give you something, especially if that something is knowledge.

One of my customers asked if I would be willing to do a workshop for their communications employees at a reduced rate. They wanted me to teach them how to go out and create their own videos. The reaction of my staff was incredulous when I told them we were going to train a roomful of people to concept and shoot their own videos. Wasn't that taking business away from us? Why would we want to share the secrets and expertise that we had amassed over so many years? Would they even need us anymore? All those were really good questions. Some might say we were working our way out of a job—I thought just the opposite.

One of my staff and I presented the workshop, and the results were amazing. Yes, the attendees did learn a lot about how to be do-it-yourselfers, and they went out and started to shoot more of their own video. But something else happened. They started to realize that, while they could do some of the production on their own, they still needed us for the really important or complicated projects. In fact, less than a week after the training session, my phone started to ring with requests for us to work on new projects. A number of them were projects that we would handle from start to finish. Others were projects where they would do some of the work, and we would handle the more complex tasks. What is the bottom line here? Our overall business with this customer has increased because of what we gave them.

Even if you have a tangible product, you still have knowledge to give away. Can you help your customer or potential customer use the product more effectively or help them reduce their costs? Can you share some of your best practices? Whatever you can give away in terms of knowledge gets your customer more engaged with you and generally results in more business.

Who Is a Great Target for a Giveaway?

Once you've decided what to give away, you'll want to develop a clear picture of who to target. Obviously, the people who have expressed an interest in your product or service are no-brainers. But you need to look at whether or not there is potential there for long-term business.

We have a profile that we have developed over the years of what our ideal customer looks like. In our case, it is a company that is forward-thinking, has ongoing needs that will bring us business at least several times a year (preferably more), and who wants a long-term relationship. When we do a giveaway, we look first to see if the company matches our ideal customer profile. We also look at doing giveaways for our existing customers that might encourage them to buy products and services that they are not currently using.

When Do You Give Something Away?

The most common time to do a giveaway is when you are trying to get the potential big customer in your door. But giveaways are also appreciated when your customer is facing difficult times. Many of our large customers have faced significant challenges during the economic downturn; they have closed facilities and reduced their workforce. They simply don't have the resources that were once available.

In one case, we got a heads-up that our client was in dire straits and was preparing to slash budgets. We decided to be proactive and asked for a meeting. We offered to help them figure out the best way to use the budget they did have, even though it was significantly less than the previous year. By leveraging some existing assets and discounting our time, we were able to provide a plan that would help them continue to market their products. We were essentially giving away some of our time. Is that smart? Should we have held out for a customer that was able to pay full price for our services? It's a judgment call, because once you discount, you may not be able to get back to charging full price.

In this case, however, the strategy worked. We helped our customer through a difficult time. As business improved and budgets got bigger, we got the business back. It can be risky to give away too much, but it can also cement and grow a relationship. It's amazing what kind of reaction you get when you give away something to big customers who are used to paying for everything as a line item. Best of all, you not only get their business, you may also get recommended to their circle of suppliers and colleagues.

But one word of caution, there are risks in giving away too much and simply hoping it will turn into long-term business. There are times when you can and should be paid for time spent doing research and development.

Giving Back

Finally, there is another type of giveaway: giving back to the larger community. For many large companies, making the world a better place is a part of their mission, their corporate DNA. These companies often have formal programs and volunteer opportunities for their employees. Smaller entities, like mine, also believe in giving back. This can be part of your legacy as you begin to think about exiting your business.

We routinely give away media production services to nonprofit organizations in our area. Or provide them at a very reduced rate. I also believe in giving time to nonprofits because sometimes that is even more valuable than the check you write. In my case, I have served and continue to serve on nonprofit boards. Bringing my business and communications expertise to them, I have been told, is invaluable.

Sometimes, our large customers ask us to support causes they support. That's great because it gives us the chance to connect on a different level. Beware, however, that you shouldn't invest in your community just to get noticed. And don't expect that it will come back to you, as often it does not. If you do this simply to strengthen current relationships, you may be disappointed. And, yes, some people will take advantage of your kind and generous spirit. But I believe that giving back helps you think outside of yourself. It provides an outlet for people's talents and, without getting too sappy, it just feels good.

I am not alone. Remember Linda Schlesinger-Wagner, CEO of skinnytees? Her small company is a powerhouse when it comes to making an impact for women and children. The company has sponsored Picture of Hope, a nonprofit that works to change the lives of homeless children in five cities. The kids get digital cameras and are taught how to take photos that "capture their hopes and dreams." The images are sold, and the proceeds go to homeless shelters.

Schlesinger-Wagner also supports breast cancer–awareness projects and tries to offer comfort and convenience with styles that have been designed to fit during treatment, when women might have heavy bandages. Trying to find something that women can wear during treatment is not top of mind for some clothing manufacturers, but it is for skinnytees. Schlesinger-Wagner says:

> We're a small company. We're giving back all the time. We're giving products to people; we're helping raise funds by matching donations. It costs us money. But do we care? No, because it feels good to

everyone on my staff and the team here. We're making a difference. And isn't that what it is all about? I think the world has forgotten that. We have to remember, there's always people that need a helping hand.[1]

TIPS TO SUCCEED

▸ Find creative ways to give potential and current customers something of value.

▸ When you give something for free, or through discount, be sure that you have assessed the potential opportunities—otherwise you might be wasting the effort.

▸ Understand the risks of sharing your intellectual property.

▸ Giving back to the community is a great way to connect on a whole different level with new audiences, but don't do it unless you really believe in the effort.

20

GET BIGGER OR STAY SMALL. IT AFFECTS YOUR EXIT.

G rowth. It is what every business owner desires. If fact, we measure ourselves by how much we grow year over year. But the decision to expand every year has consequences. When you first start a business, you are just trying to exist. That's not easy. We know that most businesses don't make it past this phase. If they do, the business goes into survival mode. Can you generate enough money to stay afloat and keep investing?

Success is intoxicating. People want what you make or provide. Your reputation grows. You hire more people, expand your portfolio. Maybe buy a building, as I did, to house your operation. Customers refer others to you, and you finally feel like you can breathe. Your business is not just surviving, it is thriving. The next phase is "take-off." Your business soars to new levels. But before you get too excited, you might want to hit the pause button. Let's explore:

- ▶ How small is small?
- ▶ Building the infrastructure for growth
- ▶ Three things to consider if you want to grow
- ▶ Understanding the choices

The definition of a small business, according to the Small Business Administration (SBA), is determined by either the average number of employees over the past twelve months or average annual receipts over the past three years. It might surprise you to know that a business is considered "small" if it has no more than fifteen hundred employees. To many, that is a pretty big number. When it comes to average annual receipts, the SBA has size standards for specific industries. To designate what industry a company falls into, you can look up a "classification code" in the North American Industry Classification System, or NAICS.

As a small-business owner, it is important that you think about how big you want to be. Do you want to have twenty-five employees? Fifty employees? Maybe fifteen hundred employees? Do you want to get bigger? How big? Stay small? How small? It is a dilemma that many businesses face. It has been said that if your business is not growing, it's dying. This, however, is a complete oversimplification of a very complex issue. Without question, when it comes to growth, there is no one easy answer for businesses. Just Google "grow your business," and you can see that there is a great deal of emphasis on growth and little talk about staying small. There are many strategies for growth, everything from getting deeper penetration with existing customers (one of my favorites), to attracting big customers, to franchising. Your type of business will, in large part, dictate which strategy to pursue.

One thing is certain, if you want to grow so that you can reap the benefits when you exit, you need to build a machine. That means you need the infrastructure to support growth. There are lots of definitions of business infrastructure. Essentially, it is the physical and organizational structures needed for the operation of a business. Others say it is all the human resources, processes, and tools you need to ensure that you can manage your growth and be profitable. I like to keep it simple.

- ▸ What do you need to do?
- ▸ Who in your organization is going to do it?
- ▸ How can they get the work done?
- ▸ What tools do they need?
- ▸ Is there a model or some formula to use so that you can have repeatable success?

> ▶ What happens if something goes wrong? Or if you have an unexpected growth spurt?

Without infrastructure, you just can't grow or, for that matter, even run an efficient small business that wants to stay small. The infrastructure needs to be appropriate for the rate of growth that you are trying to achieve. Then you have to link all of these things together so you can consistently deliver a good product or service and keep your customers happy. When you do that, you increase sales. That usually means you need to hire more people, maybe get bigger offices or warehouses, or even turn the business into a franchising opportunity.

One terrific example of growth is Biggby Coffee. Biggby boasts that it serves the world's best coffee. I know that people's taste in coffee varies, but I must agree. The first café opened in 1995, the second two years later. The franchise took off and now has over 360 locations open in thirteen states. The growth was no accident. Cofounder and co-CEO Bob Fish said he knew from the very start that he wanted to grow. Some of this can be chalked up to personality. Fish is admittedly ADHD and, like most entrepreneurs, gets bored easily. He knew that he was much more than a manager. And he did not want to do the same thing over and over again. That meant that unlike his competitors, he needed to build more than a one-operation shop.

Fish is a dreamer and when he dreams, he dreams *big*. In fact, he believed that one day he would be bigger than Starbucks. His vision from the early days was to be the largest US-franchise specialty coffee shop in America. In 2022, Biggby Coffee was one of just thirty-eight award-winning franchise companies named by Franchise Business Review in its 2022 report on the "Top Food and Beverage Franchises."

Fish said:

> We started off with one location, so there was a time I was a shopkeeper. Then I was running five units and that became twenty. That would sort of qualify me as a regional manager. There is a learning curve of leadership that has to constantly grow. The things that made me a good shopkeeper are not what make me now a good co-CEO or a good cofounder. I've had to learn new things, and I've had to learn a lot about myself in order to learn those new things.[1]

Most entrepreneurs who choose growth learn one lesson that Fish learned very quickly. You can't grow if you are at the heart of everything that happens within your organization. Taking your business from survival mode to the higher levels requires self-awareness, systems, and vision. Fish said:

> EOS [Entrepreneurial Operating System] has entered our life, and that's been great for the productivity of entrepreneurial organizations. But we are also moving towards stakeholder management, where we're trying to make decisions that are a win-win for the consumer, the owner-operator, the vendor. We had to let go of the autocratic stage, running the business with an iron fist, which didn't really allow the company to grow. It was destructive from a management perspective. We were founder managed, and that comes with such a weight of influence, such large personalities, that it doesn't really allow anybody else to grow.

> We've been very intentional, since about 2014, to begin to build the leadership team. And the leadership team is the one that's running the company, allowing us to be visionaries, allowing us to dive in more deeply on both purpose and vision. That is taking the company someplace that's really interesting and beyond just selling a cup of coffee.[2]

The vision is lofty. Fish wants to grow the company from $250 million to $1 billion by 2028 and at the same time improve the culture of the workplace in America. Fish said:

> Our system is the Petri dish. We have a white paper, so to speak, and Biggby Coffee is the experiment. It's meant to be noticed and notable. We want to be able to achieve, not on some small scale where it's cute and quaint, but grow a company of scale, care for people, and improve workplace culture.[3]

To that end, Biggby has seven core operational values, and they have not changed to this day. They are:

1. Simplicity through systems: having a system makes it teachable.

2. Be top-line driven because revenue solves all problems; to focus on the top line is to focus on the customer. After all, there is no bottom line without a top line.

3. Energy, excitement, and enthusiasm: it's how you move forward in the world.

4. Always have faith, confidence, and courage. You have to believe in yourself, or no one else will.

5. Maintain long-term sustainability through profitability; profitability is a choice, and it's the only choice that ensures sustainability.

6. Engaging the community; giving is getting.

7. Be defined by your dedication, dependability, and desire—an insatiable hunger to improve.

Those values have driven the company's success and growth. But Bob Fish is not content to just *grow* Biggby Coffee. Fish and his wife, Michelle, are on a journey to travel the world in search of coffee that brings people together and serves the planet. The initiative is "One BIGG Island in Space." It will source coffee directly from sustainable farmers around the world. The company is partnering with these farmers, helping them grow their operations. Biggby is encouraging and rewarding these farmers for running humane, sustainable, and high-quality operations by purchasing directly from them. The goal is for his franchises to serve 50 percent farm-direct coffee by 2023 and 100 percent over the following years. In the end, everyone grows—farmers, franchisees, and Biggby. Not to mention, they are helping communities thrive.

Three Things to Consider If You Want to Grow

If you choose to grow, you must have a high degree of focus on the specific things that will carry your business to the next level. That means you need to make choices. How can you be productive? Are you focused on the "right things"? Or are you caught up in the minutia?

Next, as a business owner, you simply can't do everything. And you certainly can't do what you did when you were a much smaller organization. There just isn't enough time, and you get pulled in so many different directions. You need to do that thing that so many business owners hate—delegate. Just because you *can* do something does not mean that you *should* do it. Honestly, this took me years to learn for a number of reasons: I loved doing the work; I could do things faster than my staff; I could see the results of my work immediately. That is not the case when you are working on long-term strategy, vision, and potential exit. You need to remember a lesson that Bob Fish offered. Step aside from day-to-day operations, and let others grow into the job and help grow the company.

Finally, while you should not compromise when it comes to the quality of the product, you might need to make other compromises if you want to grow. You might have to narrow your product line, outsource some of the activities, or simply not do some things.

We have all seen those stories about the "fastest-growing companies." They are on the covers of magazines one year and gone the next. Why? Maybe it was a miscalculation or some unforeseeable event. But maybe, just maybe, something else is occurring. Something that Bob Fish says is all too common: "If your ego drives your need to expand, you might lose. If there are strong economic reasons, that is our preferred method of growth."[4]

A Different Choice

Biggby Coffee is focused on growth and making every single store profitable, but I know of many small businesses that make a very different choice. They choose to stay small. They are interested in solid, steady, and measured growth, but it's not what drives them. They want to keep greater control of the product. They do not want to build lots of infrastructure or have multiple facilities or operations to manage. They don't want to constantly have to seek out new customers who require them to make more capital investments and hire many more people. In effect, these small-business owners don't want to build a machine that needs to be fed. But just because you choose to stay small does not mean that you can't do big business.

From the start, I made a conscious effort to think about how big I wanted to grow my company. What would be my ideal size? Was it fifteen employees, more than twenty, or less than fifty? Would staying small let me be choosier about customers? Could it give me more freedom? Could I actually be more profitable doing less work? Many of the small businesses in the US today are one- or two-person shops. I started out that way and now have grown to ten employees. We continue to add staff because I know that will impact my ability to do new and different things and enable my eventual exit.

Choosing to stay small has an impact on every aspect of the business, from the relationships you have with employees and customers to the control you have over the product—not to mention the amount of money you need to generate in order to keep the business healthy and moving forward.

Let's start with control. I admit I am a bit of a control freak; I like to have my hands in all different aspects of the business. When I first started, I did it all. I was selling, writing, going on location to do the interviews, and even editing. I knew, though, that I could not continue to do that. However, I still wanted to have personal contact with each client. I wanted to be able to design, create, and influence projects. It's a simple fact that the bigger you get, the more removed you become from the actual work.

When I started to hire employees, I did not need to "wear all the hats"; I was able to offload some of the tasks. Generally, they were the things that were predictable and did not require my high level of expertise. I still got to do the fun parts of the work, and with only a few employees, I did not end up spending all of my time managing people. I had the time to really focus on our customers. I could spend the time I needed to turn out the best product, instead of feeling under pressure to just get it done. I can visit a customer site, do the research I need, and get to know the people and the companies with which we work.

As we have added more employees, I have tried to hire people who are not only very skilled and talented but also self-directed. By staying small, I can interact with every person, every day. I don't need to have a gatekeeper who manages my schedule—I control it. I also like the environment of a small company where everyone knows everyone else. They like one another and spend time together outside work. Every employee also knows a little something about every current project. If a customer calls, they can answer questions and help them solve issues.

Some bigger companies achieve that small-company environment by limiting the size of their facilities. Take, for example, a company that has a group of engineers working on a project. As new projects come in and they need to add people, they don't expand that location; rather, they open a new one. This helps people stay connected and be more engaged. For us, the bottom line is that staying small helps us to provide very personalized service.

Another benefit is that we don't have to load up our schedules to keep everyone busy. I know companies that take on projects that they don't want because they are not at capacity. Let's face it, you don't want people sitting around or equipment idle. You can be really efficient—lean and mean— when you have a core set of capabilities and stick to doing only that work. If you choose to stay small, you probably don't need a big sales force or lots of leads to fill up the pipeline. You need a few really good, big, solid customers that like your work.

Whether you choose to get big or stay small, there are some things that are a given. You still have to deliver a quality product every time. You have to stay relevant; you have to keep it fresh; and you have to be profitable. Staying small doesn't mean your bottom line is small. Stay small? Get bigger? You choose—but don't just *let* it happen; instead, *make* it a thoughtful choice. And know that the choice you make will impact your exit.

TIPS TO SUCCEED

- ▸ What are the advantages and disadvantages to your business if you choose to stay small? Make a "pros and cons" list.

- ▸ What are the advantages and disadvantages to your business if you choose to grow? Make a "pros and cons" list.

- ▸ Is there anything preventing you from growing the business? Determine the obstacles and move them out of the way.

- ▸ Do you have the right infrastructure to support the business, whether it is big or small? If not, consult experts and/or your advisors for help.

21

DO YOU STILL HAVE PASSION FOR THE BUSINESS?

When you first start your business, there is excitement, a sense of pride, a passion for what you are creating or growing. There's nothing like the excitement of launching that first product or service, your first sale, signing your first big contract. Someone believes in what you are doing.

As time goes on, you begin to make connections, hire employees that take you to the next level with customers. If you are good, your business skyrockets, and there are so many things to keep you excited. Not to mention, you make it past that magic five-year mark when most businesses fail. From time to time, you do feel the full weight of the commitment it takes to be successful. After all, you can't be continually upbeat and engaged.

All businesses go through cycles. The classic business cycle goes something like this. You open the doors and experience expansion. At some point, business peaks then usually it starts to contract somewhat. Then you hit a trough that is hopefully followed by more expansion. Put simply, every business has ups and downs. Yes, there are times when the work is difficult but the passion to succeed is stronger. And when you encounter a difficult situation and solve it, it is worth the effort. In fact, you quickly forget the pain.

Surveys often show that even during difficult times, owners are amazingly passionate and positive about their businesses. They are willing to do whatever it takes. I took out a loan using the equity in my house and signed a personal guarantee.

Of course, that might not have been the best idea, but it was required to put the business on solid ground. And that drive to succeed gives you an edge against the competition. I mentioned early on in this book that I wish I had just a dime for every time someone said to me, "You really love what you do." After all my years in business, I believe even more strongly that passion is often the reason that people succeed in the face of what seems like unbelievable odds.

A Passion for Entrepreneurs

The Edward Lowe Foundation, as we discussed earlier, is focused on second-stage businesses. Through a variety of programs—from peer-to-peer learning, leadership education, and other strategic programs—they help companies continue to grow. Over the years, they have worked with countless entrepreneurs. As a result, they know firsthand their strengths and challenges. Colleen Killen-Roberts, VP of entrepreneurship, says:

> Entrepreneurs often sleep, eat, and dream about the business. The business is a reflection of themselves, and they largely get their identity from it. So it's a very scary concept for them to think about going away from it, because then who are they? It is difficult for entrepreneurs to even start thinking about this. When is the right time? Do they even have the time to think about the future? And if they do have the time, do they have the mental space to take the necessary steps. The right time is different for every person.[1]

Why Passion Wanes

Timing is important. While passion might have been the driver for years, times change. Why? There are many reasons. Perhaps the work has become routine, and that can lead to boredom. Are you bored?

When I worked in broadcasting, the decision to leave and start my own business was due in great part to a sense of boredom. I lost my passion for the work. I started to feel as though every project was one that I had tackled before. Much like the movie *Groundhog Day*—where the same thing happened day after day—there was little excitement. That's not to say I was always bored. There were things that I still found interesting and engaging, but I started to see the scales tip. The percentage of time that I spent on what I considered challenging versus boring was getting smaller.

The Financial Reward

Another reason that business owners lose their passion is financial. The business is simply not making the money needed to sustain them. It's easy to have passion when sales are soaring. But when they level out or fall, the business owner may be left feeling underappreciated and overextended.

There is no doubt that the COVID-19 pandemic permanently changed the financial picture for many. With more and more people working from home or in a more casual setting, the need to dry-clean clothes plummeted, severely impacting many small operations. Some smaller restaurants that depended on larger workplaces for their customers also saw the breakfast and lunch business disappear. These are just two examples. When businesses face this type of financial stress, it leaves owners wondering why they should continue to give it their all—so their passion fades.

People Change and So Do Priorities

Finally, people change. What once excited you now leaves you feeling empty. You loved the interaction with customers. Now it is an effort. In the past, you were energized to work through a new product introduction. Now you just don't care as much. Perhaps your priority is to spend more time with family. Or your interests have changed. This is not uncommon. What is common? People continue to work for years doing something they no longer love.

Assess Your Feelings

Being honest about how you feel is hard. In fact, it can be devastating to admit that this business that you love so much no longer excites you. It may depress you to think that you have spent so much effort on the business only to lose the spark that brought you so much joy.

You can try to fake it, go through the motions, but you may only be fooling yourself. People around you know when your heart and mind are not present. Sometimes they know it before you even identify the feelings and emotions. Employees sense your lack of urgency. Where once you would have dived into a new task or challenge, now you are not so motivated. You no longer have the desire to work with that client you used to love. Issues that used to challenge you to find solutions now annoy you.

We all know that passion ebbs and flows. There are things you can do to get it back. Pay attention. When passion does not rebound, it is a sign that you should be considering an exit. The following questions are designed to get you thinking about the level of passion that you currently have for your business.

- ▶ When it comes to your business, what are you still passionate about?
- ▶ Have you really lost your passion, or are you simply burned out?
- ▶ What do you resent at work that used to bring you joy?
- ▶ Are those activities critical to the growth of the business?
- ▶ What happens if you are unable to delegate those activities to others?
- ▶ Can you take a step back from the business to rekindle your passion?
- ▶ Are other interests more appealing?
- ▶ Do you want to spend more time with family and friends? Travel?
- ▶ Do you want to volunteer for an organization that is near and dear to your heart?
- ▶ What percentage of the time do you feel good about the work?
- ▶ How does that compare with last year or the year before? Is there a trend?

TIPS TO SUCCEED

- Passion for your business is something that naturally ebbs and flows. Assess your true feelings.

- A business owner's passion for the business is infectious. A lack of passion can also be passed on to employees and customers. Assess if your attitude is impacting your employees. If it is, try to offload some of the activities that are causing the stress. Do more of what makes you happy.

- Without a financial reward, it is difficult to continue working long hours without feeling resentful. Consider getting involved with a program like the Entrepreneurial Operating System or your local economic development center.

22
STEP OUT
AND INTO
THE NEXT
ADVENTURE

I n chapter 20, we looked at why people choose to significantly grow a business or stay smaller. When it comes to stepping out of a business, people also make choices. Some want to retire early. Some later. Some not at all—remember Bob Fish from Biggby Coffee. The truth is that one way or another, we all exit at some point. People start and grow businesses for vastly different reasons. Many do it to create a job that provides them with a certain lifestyle. Others to create a legacy or to pass it down to family members. Serial entrepreneurs start a business to grow and sell it quickly. How do your choices impact your ability to step out?

In more ways than you know; and for those thinking of stepping out, things have been changing over the past ten years.

Three Impactful Drivers

Kenneth Marks, a mergers and acquisitions advisor who focuses on smaller companies, is the managing partner of High Rock Partners, a boutique investment bank in Raleigh, North Carolina, and he's the lead author of *Middle Market M&A: Handbook for Advisors, Investors, and Business Owners*. According to Marks, there are three drivers that are making an impact. Marks said:

> The first one is generational, the wave of baby boomers retiring. The second, and probably the biggest one, is the prevalence of private equity. Private equity has become part of the alternative investment class. It's an accepted portfolio component for all your pension funds. It's a way to add to an otherwise traditional stocks-and-bonds portfolio. There's a tremendous amount of capital—$1.6 trillion—in the private equity world now that is unspent. The third is the need of the S&P 500 for earnings growth, revenue growth, and capturing new technologies in a very efficient way. Mergers and acquisitions are a proven way to—in many cases on a lower-risk basis—gain access to a particular customer base or technology or market segment. These three pillars have come together and create a very active deal market.[1]

Not sure if you are interested in exiting right now? You still should start thinking about an exit strategy. Why? If you know how you want to exit, it will help you determine how to continue to build, operate, and run your business. In addition, having a plan and sound structure in place shows your business customers that you have "taken care of business." That is very important if you want to be a long-term partner with your clients.

Building an Asset

In many smaller organizations, the business owner is the "face" of the company. This can be a real strength when working with customers but can put you at a disadvantage when it comes time to sell. As the business owner, you develop strong relationships with employees and customers. What would happen if you were gone tomorrow? Would your customers still want to work with the company? Would they trust the quality of the work? If you are running a lifestyle business and are not concerned about a sale, then it may not matter. However, if you are building an investment, an asset that appreciates, Kenneth Marks has some words of caution.

There's a lot more awareness of how companies perform than there was ten years ago or twenty years ago because there's more information and greater access to data. An owner may be making a tremendous amount of money in the business. They're enjoying the current investment, the current cash flow out. But they are not reinvesting so that the business has enterprise value separate from them. You need a clear strategy of where you're going and how you fit in the market. You need to build a team, along with repeatable and scalable systems. If you don't invest in those things, you will not have an asset that can be sold at a premium in the future. I've seen this before where a company may be [worth] a hundred million dollars, but it's run by an owner that is doing everything. There is no management team. They lead everything. When they leave or die, the company falls apart. There is not a lot of value in it.[2]

The Team of Advisors

The "strategy" that Marks referred to is critical. Just as you need a team of advisors at start-up, you need a team to help with your exit strategy. Business owners usually have the typical team that includes accountants, attorneys, insurance professionals, and others. But many wait too long to enlist help from a wealth advisor. I know what you are thinking. "I can manage this on my own." Or "I have a stockbroker." Great, but a wealth advisor is very different from a broker. They take a holistic approach, and outside help is invaluable to keep from making some typical errors.

Tom Price, of Hungerford Financial, made this observation:

I find that business owners put a lot of their cash back into their business. That is a good thing. But sometimes they amass too much of their wealth in their practice, or in their business, versus taking some of that cashflow and investing it in other things for diversification. This strategy could add additional risks to a successful retirement. I like to see business owners work on a proper diversification structure at least five years before they decide to retire.[3]

Kenneth Marks echoes that concept and offers this perspective for those who choose a different path.

How does your business fit into your portfolio of what will eventually be your assets? If you're taking all the cash today and actually investing it, that can be a very reasonable strategy. You might not want to build your business with a lot of inherent value. You might just want the cash today to reinvest. The classic example I hear from owners is one using the cash cow to buy real estate. Maybe the owner does not want to invest in the long-term future value of business. Maybe they don't have enough confidence in the market or their ability to compete. That happens all the time. And that's okay. But if you have that approach, it's nice when it is an intentional strategy and not just something you fall into because you have to do it.[4]

A Framework for Sellers

To make sure you are intentional, you need expert guides, such as a tax accountant and an attorney that is familiar with selling companies. And a team lead. That's what Marks and firms like his do. Marks has a framework for sellers that is clear and actionable. It is called a "quadra-cycle"—a circular and iterative way of thinking that takes into account four domains. The first is obvious. Why do you or your family own the business? We already discussed the difference between a lifestyle business and one that you grow for social and financial reasons.

The other three domains are more complicated. Marks explains:

Number two in the decision process is understanding the industry of the company. And where is it in the life cycle of the industry? Are you an industry that is just starting to take off and well positioned? Or in a mature industry? You need to know that because that plays a big piece in decision-making. In fact, when we've done some surveys and research, market timing for where you are in the industry is actually the number one driver. It is also a big driver of value.

Number three is the business cycle. This is talking about the broad economy. Everyone's talking now about a recession versus a bull market. Coming out of 2008 and 2009, there were a lot of people that wanted to sell and a whole generation that thought they would sell. And they couldn't and had to weather the next seven years till the market recovered. We have heard people say, "I don't want to go through that again. I want to get out now while the getting is good, so to speak."[5]

The final domain is the classic strengths and weaknesses of the business. Think about a SWOT analysis: Strengths, Weaknesses, Opportunities, Threats. Working with a professional, you can discuss and see the implications of the four areas; why you own the business, the position in the industry, the business cycle, and the strengths and weaknesses of the business. Marks summed it up this way:

Take a company that is in a hot market and that is not run very well. That could be attractive. You may be better off selling them now when they can get sold. When the market's not hot and a company is not performing very well, you are not going to be able to sell them at all.[6]

The question is not *do you need help* in stepping out but *who is going to lead* the engagement and what is their process? I get many calls and emails from business brokers. They start by saying they have interested buyers and offer to do an analysis of your business. Some of these organizations do seminars in cities all across the country to pitch their services. These organizations sell businesses like real estate agents sell houses. They may be the perfect fit for smaller businesses who may not need the skills of a more sophisticated advisor. Marks's firm works with mergers and acquisitions in the five- to fifty-million-dollar range. Here, the landscape is very different. As companies get over one hundred million dollars, they typically hire an investment banker with a team to help them run the sales process.

The numbers will dictate the type of broker or advisor that is right for you. However, you still need to look carefully at the choices within that group of advisors, because each type has a "sweet spot." Ask the advisor to articulate their process and the type of clients they serve. There are some businesses that really need a specialist to lead the sale. Do you own a highly technical business or a niche business that has a language all its own? In that case, you need someone who understands the industry and probably knows the likely buyers.

Another important consideration is your point of contact for the engagement. While you may be tempted to go with a larger, well-known firm, that may not be the best option. Marks offers this advice:

> More important than the firm name is the partner that is going to own the process for you. If you can't get a straight answer on that, it is clearly not the right firm. You want to know who the partner is and how involved they will be. I'll give you an example. We get into spaces where we may compete with a bigger investment bank. The bigger investment bank is going to put the B or C team on the engagement. Would you rather have the junior B and C team from a big-name investment bank? Or would you rather get the senior guys from our side? We are going to lead it ourselves, and you get the handholding you need from a partner.[7]

Don't Get Sloppy

The one thing I have noticed among fellow business owners is the tendency to let their businesses get "out of shape" and sloppy. Some who choose not to step out try to milk as much as they can out of the company without investing too much more. What's the problem? When you let the business get old and tired, you start to lose customers, especially big ones who do business with you because you are forward-thinking and aggressive. Key employees see the lack of attention and start to worry about the future. They often pick up and move to a place that has more potential and a more secure outlook. When a business starts to decline, it is not easy to reverse the trend. So, if you decide to sit tight, pay attention, or you might not get those few extra years of income—it simply won't be there.

For those who get into selling mode, there is also a concern. During the time you are working on a sale, you really have two jobs: continue to run the business profitably and grow, and work on the sale. They are both demanding jobs. If you don't continue to keep things moving, you are likely to get overwhelmed and become fatigued. Once you decide to sell, step out, move as quickly as you can through the process, and move on to the next adventure.

The Next Adventure

As a business owner, I sometimes find it difficult to explain to others why I continue to work. I get lots of questions.

- ▸ "Why are you still working if you have enough money to retire?"
- ▸ "Do you think you will retire to Florida, which is where your siblings retired?"
- ▸ "Don't you get tired of all the travel?"

The list of inquiries goes on. So why do I continue to work? My explanation is that I love what I do. I can't imagine waking up without a to-do list or a schedule of activities. I am still excited about the work and clients. But if I really delve into it, I must admit that I have not yet thoroughly defined my next adventure. I am working on a plan, and that is a good thing, because too many owners are left floundering after the sale of their business.

Tom Price of Hungerford Financial has seen this firsthand. Price says:

I have had owners that sold their businesses and then wished they had not. Over the years, the business became their life, and they grew accustomed to moving at a hundred miles an hour to keep it going. Additionally, the business is what brought them joy. Without the benefit of outside activities or hobbies, they had a difficult time adjusting to not being a busy owner. So now I address this with people and ask them to think through what they are going to do when they sell the company.[8]

That is advice that many do not get when considering a sale.

Two Tales of Adventure

Yan Ness, a former owner of Online Technology, was one of those business owners who moved at a hundred miles an hour and rarely slept much when running his company. When he struck a deal to sell, he was not prepared for the fact that the new owner did not want him to stay on for a transition period. Ness said:

> They brought in their own CEO. It was the most emotional period. That was tough, honestly. It was like, wait a minute. . . . How can you just take the keys to this big, expensive machine and drive it by yourself? How can you not have the captain show you the shutoff switch? Ask me to come to a couple of meetings? Nope, boom, you are out of here. Gone. And that hurt. But here's the thing. Twenty-five years ago, I made a goal. I wanted someday to sell a business that had so much intrinsic value that it would run without me. So, I was conflicted.[9]

In the run up to the sale, Ness was busy maximizing the value, making sure that customers and employees were cared for, and managing communications. In hindsight, he believes he should have budgeted some time to think about what was next. For a week after "turning in the keys," he slept ten hours a night. He never slept that much while running the company.

What Ness did next is very typical. He aggressively took on the challenge of retirement. He moved onto his boat and went sailing for three months. Then it was off to Italy for five weeks. There was more travel. Lots of reading and, of course, bingeing on Netflix.

> After about six months, I got really bored. The kids were gone. We didn't have a dog. I had nothing to do. Judy had already retired, so she was doing art and cooking. She's got friends, she's doing twenty different things. I was doing nothing. It was bad. Then you start thinking about legacy and purpose. I would literally go to bed and be upset with myself.[10]

Today, Ness has found his purpose. He is the CEO of a company that he invested in called VergeIO. Ness says he has finally found the balance he needs to work and live a fuller life.

> I'm just not very good at filling my time. I don't have very many hobbies. I felt like I should exercise this brain muscle again. And so I'm having a ton of fun. I get to work with smart, driven people. And it's by far the biggest opportunity I've ever had. It could be just incredibly transformative. Best of all, it is right up my alley. I get the industry

and have a good Rolodex. So, it's fun when you feel like you're in a position to win.[11]

By contrast, Vicki and Charles Phaneuf of Raleigh, North Carolina, sold CE Rental, a business that they had grown over twenty years, with no regrets. Vicki said:

> It was the best decision we ever made. The timing was perfect, and I would not have done anything differently. I guess when it is right, it is right. The day we sold it was sad, really hard to believe that it was over. I cried. But when the money went into the bank, I smiled. We celebrated our anniversary and the sale of the business at the same time. I asked Charles, what are you getting me next year for our anniversary?[12]

The couple did stay on for six months but say that ninety days would have been better. Like most business owners, they did not agree with all the decisions that were being made. That is common. As Charles said, "It was not ours anymore, so we suggested but did not insert ourselves into their business. It was hard to watch. But we left the business in good condition, and it has survived. That makes us feel proud."[13]

When they walked out the door for good, they were relieved. Today the Phaneufs are literally "sitting on a beach" and have this to offer to those considering a sale.

> Some say the money is not important. It is, especially if you have years to live on your retirement funds. We wanted to be financially secure and be able to help others. It is also important to be emotionally ready, so that when you are done . . . you are done! You do not want to have regrets.[14]

Find the Balance

Have you thought about your next adventure? Perhaps it is travel. Spending more time with family. Starting a new business. Volunteering. For every person, the answer will be different. But one thing is sure, you need to ask the question. It is an emotional one.

As business owners and executives, we have been taught to take emotion out of decisions. I would argue that this is one decision where emotion is critical. That is not to say we should let it take over, but it certainly is a consideration. We need to balance emotion with good decision-making so that we can do what is profitable for the business but can also make sure to feed our souls.

TIPS TO SUCCEED

▸ Operate your business like you're going to sell it; keep your house in order and be prepared for opportunities.

▸ Have good financial information. Use an outside accountant to double-check your numbers; do not cut corners. Stay in compliance with tax filings and close each year cleanly (from a financial point of view).

▸ Build your business with customers and employees that a buyer would want to inherit.

NOTES

Chapter 1

1. Jennifer Post. "Companies Founded by Amazing Young Entrepreneurs." Business News Daily online (February 21, 2023), *businessnewsdaily.com*.
2. Linda Schlesinger-Wagner. Interview by author, April 2023.
3. Ibid.
4. Marilyn D. Landis. Interview by author, February 2013.
5. John Kowalski. Interview by author, February 2013.
6. Ibid.
7. Jack Buchanan. Interview by author, April 2023.
8. Ibid.
9. Mark Peters. Interview by author, January 2013.

Chapter 2

1. Bob Fish. Interview by author, January 2013.
2. Bob Fish. Interview by author, March 2022.

Chapter 3

1. Tracy Brower. Interview by author, April 2022, *tracybrower.com*.
2. Ibid.
3. Elma Mrkonjić. "Job Satisfaction Statistics: How Important Is It for Americans." Seed Scientific online (October 15, 2021), *seedscientific.com*.
4. Tracy Brower interview.
5. Colleen Killen-Roberts. Interview by author, March 2023, *edwardlowe.org*.

Chapter 5

1. National Small Business Association. "Improve Access to Capital." NSBA Issue Briefs, 2023–2024 Issue Priorities, *www.nsba.biz/issuebriefs*.
2. Sandra Jelinski. Interview by author, April 2023.
3. Marilyn Landis. Interview by author, February 2023.
4. Ibid.
5. Ibid.

6. Ibid
7. Sandra Jelinski interview.
8. Marilyn Landis, 2023 interview.
9. National Small Business Association, "Improve Access to Capital."
10. Sandra Jelinski interview.
11. National Small Business Association, "Improve Access to Capital."
12. Sandra Jelinski interview.
13. Marilyn Landis, 2023 interview.
14. Marilyn Landis. Interview by author, February 2013.
15. Marilyn Landis, 2023 interview.
16. Marilyn Landis, 2013 interview.
17. Ibid.

Chapter 6

1. Marilyn Landis. Interview by author, February 2013.

Chapter 9

1. Dan Barraclough. "The Importance of Effective Workplace Communication— Statistics," 11 Key Workplace Communication Statistics. Expert Market online (May 2022), *www.expertmarket.com.*
2. Jack Flynn. "28+ Incredible Meeting Statistics (2023): Virtual, Zoom, In-person Meetings and Productivity." Zippia online (July 6, 2023), *www.zippia.com/advice /meeting-statistics.*

Chapter 10

1. Bob Fish. Interview by author, January 2013.
2. Ibid.
3. Mark Peters. Interview by author, January 2013.
4. Charles Phanuef. Interview by author, March 2013.

Chapter 11

1. John Kowalski. Interview by author, February 2023.
2. Kate Moran. "The Four Dimensions of Tone of Voice." Nielson Norman Group (July 17, 2016), *www.nngroup.com.*
3. John Kowalski, 2023 interview.
4. Ibid.
5. Ibid.

Chapter 12

1. Mark Peters. Interview by author, January 2013.
2. Ibid.

Chapter 13

1. Marilyn Landis. Interview by author, February 2023.

Chapter 14

1. Carl Oberland. Interview by author, February 2013.
2. Mark Peters. Interview by author, January 2013.
3. Carl Oberland interview.
4. Christopher Locke. Interview by author, February 2013.
5. Ibid.
6. Ibid.
7. Ibid.
8. Ibid.
9. Claudio Knizek et al. "Why Global Industrial Supply Chains Are Decoupling," chapter 2: Rethinking Global Supply Chain Models. Earnst & Young Global Limited, *ey.com.*
10. Christopher Locke interview.
11. Ibid.

Chapter 15

1. Christopher Locke. Interview by author, February 2013.
2. John Kowalski. Interview by author, February 2013.
3. Christopher Locke interview.

Chapter 16

1. Bonnie Alfonso. Interview by author, February 2023.
2. John Kowalski. Interview by author, February 2023.
3. Bonnie Alfonso interview.
4. Ibid.
5. Mark Peters. Interview by author, January 2013.
6. John Kowalski, 2023 interview.
7. Bonnie Alfonso interview.

Chapter 17

1. Chad Paalman. Interview by author, February 2023.
2. Ibid.
3. "Average Network Administrator Salary," Payscale (updated August 15, 2023), *www.payscale.com/research/US/Job=Network_Administrator/Salary.*
4. "How Much Does a Network Administrator Make?," Glassdoor (updated August 30, 2023), *www.glassdoor.com/Salaries/network-administrator-salary -SRCH_KO0,21.htm.*

5. Chad Paalman interview.

6. National Institute of Standards and Technology, US Department of Commerce, NIST Standards, *www.nist.gov*.

7. Chad Paalman interview.

8. See *chat.openai.com*.

9. Chad Paalman interview.

10. "2022 Data Breach Investigations Report," Verizon, *www.verizon.com*.

11. Chad Paalman interview.

12. Ibid.

Chapter 18

1. John Kowalski. Interview by author, February 2013.

Chapter 19

1. Linda Schlesinger-Wagner. Interview by author, April 2023.

Chapter 20

1. Bob Fish. Interview by author, March 2022.

2. Ibid.

3. Ibid.

4. Bob Fish. Interview by author, January 2013.

Chapter 21

1. Colleen Killen-Roberts. Interview by author, March 2023.

Chapter 22

1. Kenneth Marks. Interview by author, November 2022.

2. Ibid.

3. Tom Price. Interview by author, March 2023.

4. Kenneth Marks interview.

5. Ibid.

6. Ibid.

7. Ibid.

8. Tom Price interview.

9. Yan Ness. Interview by author, March 2022.

10. Ibid.

11. Ibid.

12. Vicki Phaneuf. Interview by author, April 2022.

13. Charles Phaneuf. Interview by author, April 2022.

14. Vicki and Charles Phaneuf interview.

INDEX

ABOUT THE AUTHOR

Cynthia Kay (CK) is the founder of Cynthia Kay and Company, a top-tier, award-winning communications and media production company; she is also an author, speaker, and recognized expert in small-business leadership.

CK's small-business expertise is a result of her decades of experience after starting and building her own company. Today, her firm's clients range from small innovative start-ups to nonprofits to Global Fortune 100 companies and in industries as diverse as manufacturing, technology, publishing, and healthcare. Over her career, CK's success has been widely recognized. She was named "Woman-Owned Small-Business Supplier of the Year" by Siemens in 2018 and "One of the 50 Most Influential Women in West Michigan" five times. She earned "101 Best Companies of West Michigan" twice and "Top Women-Owned Business in Michigan" four times.

CK has contributed her knowledge and experience to numerous boards, including chair of the National Small Business Association (NSBA), board chair of Small Business Association of Michigan (SBAM), and chair of Legislative Action Committee of Small Business Association of Michigan. She is an active board member of Michigan Celebrates Small Business, which awards the "50 Companies to Watch."

CK speaks nationally on small-business management, communication, and women in business. Having deep experience in all these areas, she is extremely well equipped to speak to audiences about their issues in their language, offering them insightful, actionable, practical recommendations to solve their most pressing issues. As an expert in communication and small-business management, she has been featured in such publications as *Time Magazine, Entrepreneur Magazine's* Ask the Expert, the *Washington Post,* the *Los Angeles Daily News,* the *Denver Post,* and the *Boston Herald* and has appeared on NPR, NBC, and CBS affiliates.

CK began her career as an investigative journalist, during which time she received over thirty broadcast awards from UPI, AP, and Detroit Press Club between 1980 and 1987. Through this analytic training, CK learned how to dig deep and ask the right questions, which has made her an outstanding thought partner for her clients and an engaging speaker for her audiences.

CK is the author of *Small Business for Big Thinkers: Unconventional Strategies to Connect with and Win Big Business* (Career Press, 2013) and co-author of *Stop Wishing. Stop Whining. Start Leading.—A No-Nonsense, Straight-Talk Guide for Women Who Aspire to Lead* (2016).

Please visit *CynthiaKayBiz.com* to learn more.

CK would love to hear from you!

To learn more about speaking, workshops, and "Quick Hit" presentations, contact her at: *CynthiaKayBiz.com/contact.*